THE MYTHOLOGY OF THE ARTIST

THE
MYTHOLOGY
OF THE
ARTIST

R. C. COSTELLO

Copyright © 2019 R. C. Costello.

All rights reserved. No part of this book may be reproduced, stored, or transmitted by any means—whether auditory, graphic, mechanical, or electronic—without written permission of both publisher and author, except in the case of brief excerpts used in critical articles and reviews. Unauthorized reproduction of any part of this work is illegal and is punishable by law.

CONTENTS

Introduction vii

Towards a new kind of artist 1

Towards a new mythology 8

Towards a new ethic 37

The two knowledges 43

Suffering and transcendence 65

Music and the body 84

Advice on creating 115

Notes 123

INTRODUCTION

This book came out of writing and recording my sixth album, *Build Again*, which itself was a culmination of a time of transition in my life. I had recently emerged from a dark time of struggling with my health. After finishing the album I found I had ideas on creativity which could be useful to put into a book. However, once I began formulating my thoughts, I realized that to write about the highest levels of artistic creativity required writing about new ways of thinking. Only a strong mythological foundation can produce great art. It feels like a new story is needed.

In this book I'm trying to describe glimmers of a new way of thinking, a new mythology that would be more holistic than what has come before, and a new way of being as an artist. I don't feel as if this is the ultimate truth, but I do know that this way of thinking can be effective. I've tried to evaluate everything against my actual experience of the world. I realize there have been endless philosophical debates over whether something like beauty even exists. However, since in my experience beauty does exist and can be profoundly affecting, I decided not to even enter the debate. So as you read you will see I am making certain assumptions, and I hope you will go along with my train of thought and see if it leads somewhere useful. I write this as an artist, not a philosopher, so I use the subjective language of poetry and metaphor.

Since I'm trying to move across disciplines of thought in philosophy, science, psychology, and art, I know I will not do justice to some things and for that I apologize in advance. This book is attempting to be practical, not technical. I'm also using the opportunity to introduce my favorite thinkers and artists, since we stand on the shoulders of giants like Julia Cameron and Abraham Maslow.

This book starts with a very wide-angle view and becomes more practical as it moves along. Near the end I share some in-depth thoughts about music and recording, as well as advice on creating, and I hope this will provide an illustration for you of the mind of the playful artist when approaching their craft. I am a flawed messenger, a product of my own journey and western upbringing. I feel fortunate to have been in a position to think deeply about life and art. We are all fellow travelers, I hope that ultimately this book is helpful on your journey.

TOWARDS A NEW KIND OF ARTIST

The role of the artist has become corrupted. In music the artist has been mythologized as the 'rock star', defiantly self-destructive on a path of excess even to the point of suicide. But the true role of the artist is as a truthteller, and the true power of art lies in story. Over the last century artists have become very good at illuminating hypocrisies and tearing down false narratives, but to what is the artist directing us towards?

The western cult of consuming lays bare before us as an empty husk, and artists have played a role both in creating it and tearing it down. The story has been told. We've accumulated all the things in the world to the point where we've nearly destroyed the world, and yet we are still not satisfied. At this point the emperor has no clothing on and everyone is aware, and we must now begin a radical shift towards a new mythology and shared set of ethics and values.

We have tremendous capacity each of us to be selfish. But true art calls us to something greater, the collective transcendent truths that reach beyond the self. That call to what is deeper is essential for a society, especially for the youth, because each generation needs an embodiment of the ideal. Artists are the only ones who can lead this movement because it will need something greater than human logic - it must be a movement of the heart and out of people's hearts. Artists are the only ones who can spin new mythology out of the depths of the unconscious.

The true artist sees that culture has a tremendous power but is also highly flexible. The artist must stand outside of culture and practice the craft. The prophet, the monk, the sufi, the seer, all are incarnations of the artist as truthteller and outsider. In a primal state in the wilderness stands the prophet, the seer, the shaman. They are found in a primal state but they are selfless. We know instinctively that true artists serve only the truth and the collective ideal, not the self.

Today we are in the infant stages of a mass experiment in connecting networks of human brains. We don't fully know the ramifications of this, although one thing immediately apparent is it permits culture to shift very quickly. Humans seem to behave like pack animals with the capacity to flow together from the depth of our psyche. A better analogy to digital capability might be a school of fish shifting together in realtime by syncing thought patterns. This makes the network extremely nimble, but cultural acceleration can be dangerous. How dangerous we do not know, because this is a novel experiment in connecting humanity in realtime. We know emotions are contagious, but we do not know how much and how far humans will go.

As digital pioneer and critic/artist Jaron Lanier has astutely foreseen, this means artists who are not connected to the network will be needed more than ever, to tell stories clearly and present mythologies.[1] Every culture is a lens through which we view the world. The lens is mythological, and the mythology is built primarily with art. Art, at its best, permits you to change lenses temporarily. It can also permit you to catch a glimpse of your own lens from a different angle, or from the outside, which can cause seismic shifts in societal thinking. Outsider artists, prophets, creating with originality and free of the network will be needed to keep culture on the bearings of what is real and true.

Art is fundamentally an exploration of one's own soul. Digital devices provide a constant stimulation and feedback, a flow of distraction. In a darkened world it can feel like a relief to remain on the surface, never to dig deep, always stimulated and distracted. But after a while the soul of the artist wears thin. Always expressing with less to express. The artist longs to dig deep into the psyche, the unconscious, the soul. That takes time and exploration. Out of that flows the raw creative material from which a living culture can be formed.

If the highest aim of the artist is producing masterful art then everything else must be subordinate. The network will exert a force towards conformity, conformity to tribes, but the artist must stand alone and original conforming only to truth. With malice towards none but also beholden to none. No great art was created to win the approval of others or to provoke others, although great art has done both. Truly transcendent art can only be created by someone deep in the world of original artistic expression. In that world creativity flows out of the unconscious unbidden, with no master, the soul in its entirety without regard to culture, even without regard to how it will be received in the lifetime of the artist.

Transcendent art simply arises up out of the soul. That's why artists are often surprised by their creations. The soul emerges as its own unique thing, new but immediately recognizable to all other souls, embodied in a unique way within the craft of its creator. Craft gives shape to soul. As American writer Flannery O'Connor said, "I write to discover what I know."[2]

The ideal of the soul is expressed with beauty. Every ancient culture, from Iran to Mexico, Japan to South Africa, holds what is beautiful in high regard through their rituals and traditions. The elevation of beauty is a near universal across geographies and timespans. Joseph Campbell, a great student and compiler of mythologies, was fond of saying beauty touches our soul in a way that is 'divinely superfluous' (taking from poet Robinson Jeffers).[3,4] Although we do express the darkest thoughts and themes, art can do that in quite beautiful ways, which weaves a thread of hope throughout the tragedy. The beauty of the opera combines with its tragic content to create a living synergy. The human story is ultimately tragic again and again, as we all are flawed mortals battling our own dragons, telling stories of flawed mortals battling dragons.

But the courageous artist does battle. A central myth of many human cultures is the hero battling the monster or dragon. We each have a dragon, probably many dragons. We were thrown into this world with family dragons, and as we've dragged ourselves out of that mud we've created dragons of our own. Some dragons we cannot look at directly, they are too awful, so we can act as if they do not exist. We look at them from our peripheral vision, or from the scene of their destruction the day after.

But dragons can only be ignored for so long. They are easier to kill when small. They are very dangerous and difficult to battle when large. We all have dragons to face, constantly. So we each have a choice - not whether we have dragons, but whether we will battle them or surrender. We have that choice every day. If we lose or surrender today there is always tomorrow. Art can show us a tomorrow, it shows the struggle, and within the beauty can show hope. Art is also a storehouse of knowledge, creativity, and emotion for future generations. It shows us alternate ways of living and being and thinking. Like pushing through the furs in the closet to find you stumbled on not only Narnia, but a whole box of Narnias.

Art opens up a world we often pretend doesn't exist. This world contains powerful primal forces, which can be harnessed for good or evil. That is why the artist must be extremely careful when opening up this world of dragons. Artists should have a hippocratic oath: first do no harm. Open up the darkest places of the human psyche to heal them, but do no further harm. We should open it to show the struggle, within the beauty of the story. The hero is the one who struggles, only the storyteller knows whether the hero in the struggle will live or die. But whether victorious or tragic the story of the journey is powerful to our psyche.

Within our unconscious is a tremendous power. Many would-be artists have been consumed by the dragon, unable to harness it but also unwilling to leave its den, they self-destruct blindly in slow-motion. The artist willingly goes into danger, into the den, but must do so with eyes wide open. Disciplined, trained, and ready to take on the dragon directly, the artist descends into the psyche with only a torch. As we study artists who came before us we see the descent is not without risk.

Western culture has created a myth of the artist as a narcissistic genius, using up muse after muse and leaving a trail of broken lives. This mode of being is both self-indulgent and self-destructive, a worship of the self and degradation of others. We've seen this mythology play out many times. Most of the western myths are at foundation selfish myths. They are myths of domination and subjugation of everything and everyone. But this is only the dragon unchained, fully indulged with no restraint. Because this incarnation of the artist inevitably self-destructs, it is neither good for the artist or society. It is a sacrifice of the future for the present: future relationships, future art, future being. It is so obviously self-destructive over time that it becomes self-evident this incarnation does not fully fulfill the archetype of the artist, prophet, poet, or mystic. It's a corruption of its form.

The true form of the artist is the seer in the watchtower, the truthteller, fully unblinded by prejudice. In Greek mythology Cassandra was a king's daughter who was cursed by the gods to be able to see far into the future but never believed. Ever-prophesying terrible things to come but never listened to, it was a wretched state of powerless knowledge. The artist too can be cursed to be able to see the end of many paths, the weight of which can be a tremendous burden. This can drive an artist to seek to drown the sorrow by self-destructing in a blitz of altering substances. The artist sees too much. Too much suffering, too much pain, too much of what's underneath each person. Like the Greek king Oedipus, some artists would rather blind themselves than have to fully face the darkness.

But the artist cannot be only the one who sees, but also must be the one who communicates what is seen with emotional power. If never communicated those visions will die with the envisioner, never spun into mythology that can be passed on. We don't know if we will become Picassos or Cassandras, celebrated culture-changers or ignored outcasts, there is really no way to know when you set on the path. Either way, the artist's best strategy is to go deep to create with emotion, and discipline oneself using craft available in the moment of time that is given.

Clarity of emotion is the seat of the artist's power. A full reckoning with the unconscious. Nothing we do must obscure its clarity. As Nietzsche said in *Twilight of the Idols*,

> Courage and freedom of feeling before a powerful enemy, before a sublime calamity, before a problem that arouses dread — this triumphant state is what the tragic artist chooses, what he glorifies.[5]

American painter Mark Rothko wrestled with abstraction, forms, and color, but he ultimately saw clarity of emotion as the goal of the artist,

> The progression of a painter's work, as it travels in time from point to point, will be toward clarity: toward the elimination of all obstacles between the painter and the idea, and between the idea and the observer…to achieve this clarity is, inevitably, to be understood.[6]

But in reality that clarity is very rare. Artists find it so difficult they often approach their emotions obliquely, with obtuse metaphors, or by taking on personas to gain some separation from their true selves. To express something outside of the current cultural lens is a brave act, and all expressions from the soul of deep emotion fall outside of the prevailing culture. A path through a dark forest not even on the current culture's map. Once an artist breaks through there is often a torrent of art breaking behind like a wave. A pent-up flood of emotion that was never being expressed by the old lens, now finding life and expression in the new.

Along with clarity of emotion can come feelings of profound vulnerability. Exposed, opened, offered as a sacrifice, and extremely vulnerable. As Madeleine L'Engle put it succinctly in *Walking on Water: Reflections on Faith and Art*, "I love, therefore I am vulnerable."[7] Young artists who cannot tolerate such vulnerability subsequently cannot achieve the clarity of emotion of a mature artist. And this is another opportunity for substance abuse, as the artist feels the vulnerability required is too great to handle without a dulling agent. "If I could only get to another emotional level," says the artist. But here again, full clarity is often obscured by the substance itself, and a new path begins to unfold of self-destruction.

Offered as a sacrifice, the artist can also start to take on the role of the messiah, suffering with drama on the road to a romantic death. But this as well is not the artist's role. The artist must simply communicate through craft with clarity. All else obscures the image. Celebrity obscures the clarity of the craft, the emotion, and the soul. Since clarity of soul is the primary goal of the artist then everything must become subordinate. If celebrity obscures the soul then celebrity is not for the true artist. In a digital society fame is another drug to binge on, to overdose on, and to self-destruct with. But a true artist will ask - what is the ultimate goal of the artist? Everything else must be forced to be subordinate. The artist must be ruthlessly focused, this is true mastery.

More than ever a new story is needed. The old stories have long been dead, and we've used them long past their expiration. And now we are like dreamers who are waking up to a world we do not recognize and are not equipped to navigate. Our old stories helped us create this world of tremendous technological complexity, but new stories are needed so we can try to traverse it. We must collectively awake now, because the time is getting late. We can afford to sleep no longer. The artists among us must shine out with originality and clarity and strike a spark into society's heart. Moral clarity is needed more than ever before. The time has come. Awake!

TOWARDS A NEW MYTHOLOGY

Some of the earliest symbolic human art comes from burials. A human has died, the body is decaying, what is unique about the deceased has departed - the breath, spirit, or what we could call soul. So we bury the body with artistic symbolism to acknowledge the soul that has left the body, and prepare it for the afterlife.

This belief is fundamentally spiritual, and it appears to be nearly universal in humans. To put it another way, it appears to be essential to being human. In *Art and Artist*, psychologist Otto Rank looks at the history of art and sees the idea of the soul as being fundamental to a society being able to create original art,

> What makes the evolution of the soul-concept, therefore, so important in an analysis of the art-problems is the fact that not only does it form the hypothesis and incentive for all creative work, but this evolution is seen to be in parallel with the origin and expression of the creative urge itself...
>
> It is precisely the concreteness of art as compared with the idea of the soul that makes it convincing; for it creates something visible and permanent in contrast to something which was merely thought or felt, which was at first handed down from one generation to another only by means of mystic tradition.[8]

The soul, acknowledged and honored in art and traditions throughout humanity's history. If we can, as a society, agree on that - the existence of a soul, a fundamentally human concept and the prerequisite for making art, then we have a foundation for a unifying mythology. Each human being is a soul, not simply a body and mind, but a soul to be reckoned with, responsible to, and responsible for. One body, one soul. This is a good foundation for a mythology, and then artists must create the texture, depth, and realism of this mythology through their art.

One body, one soul, one mind that can change, one life to be redeemed from the wreckage. This is a good starting place for a mythology. The German philosopher Heidegger said we are each 'thrown' into our bodies, at a place in the world, in a time in history not of our choosing.[9] We are each one thrown soul at a fundamental level, thrown into the churn of creation and destruction that is life, thrown into and fully dependent on an imperfect body that will slowly die. As Plato said we are each, "imprisoned in the body, like an oyster in his shell."[10] But we know the soul to be more than the body, it is something higher, more universal, and transcendent where the body is mortal.

If we believe this then we have a mythology of soul and body over time - a soul that can change and grow while the body ages, a body that decays and a soul that does not. These two components underlie all mythology, and this is what I propose is fundamentally human. The heights achieved by Greek humanism were made possible by a mythology that exalted the human soul, developed over time by Pythagoras, Socrates, Plato, and finally Plotinus.[11] "Know thyself" was the Greek philosophy condensed by Socrates into a single potent maxim. Our western Renaissance sprang from the philosophy of the Greeks, and the fertile mythology of the ancient Celts and Christianity, and then we tried to sever the tree from the root. But we cut too far, and lost what has value and meaning to us as humans.

This problem was articulated quite clearly by husband and wife writers, historians, and philosophers, Will and Ariel Durant. In the early 1900s the Durants were American emigrants and far left radicals. They fell in love in an anarchist commune in New York City called the Ferrer Modern School, where he was the Jesuit-trained principal and she was a student. The objective of the Modern School was to abolish all forms of authority and usher in a new world based on the voluntary cooperation of free individuals. The Durants left the school to marry, and eventually turned away from anarchism deciding instead to write books on the lessons of macro-history together. Their stated goal was to try to bring all of history and philosophy under a single viewpoint, so that lessons could be learned, and mistakes avoided, by future generations. They eventually wrote the joint *Dual Autobiography* about their lives together, but only after the epic eleven volume *Story of Civilization*.

The Durants felt that knowledge had become too fragmented, split, fractured, and that the goal of the modern human, with tremendous knowledge at our immediate disposal, should be to have the 'view of the divine' and understand the lessons about humanity from all of time. They acknowledged that history is simply a viewpoint, objective truth is never able to be fully known by humans, but by pulling back to a bird's-eye view and studying the large trends of history we can learn about how humans tend to behave.

They saw history as a cycle with big forces at play, especially between religion and secularism. As they described in *Story of Civilization Volume 1*,

> Hence a certain tension between religion and society marks the higher stages of every civilization. Religion begins by offering magical aid to harassed and bewildered men; it culminates by giving to a people that unity of morals and belief which seems so favorable to statesmanship and art; it ends by fighting suicidally in the lost cause of the past. For as knowledge grows or alters continually, it clashes with mythology and theology, which change with geological leisureliness. Priestly control of arts and letters is then felt as a galling shackle or hateful barrier, and intellectual history takes on the character of a "conflict between science and religion." Institutions which were at first in the hands of the clergy, like law and punishment, education and morals, marriage and divorce, tend to escape from ecclesiastical control, and become secular, perhaps profane. The intellectual classes abandon the ancient theology and—after some hesitation—the moral code allied with it; literature and philosophy become anticlerical.[12]

The Durants were very insightful at finding patterns within history. Religious forces provide the moral foundation for a unified society, which then allow secular forces to take over and achieve great heights. Eventually secular forces overreach causing a slow destruction. From their perspective, spiritual and secular forces churn in great cycles over time, like gigantic glaciers slowly moving against each other, with one or the other taking prominence, and the reverberations echoing over the generations. But what if there was a higher way? It is clear that secularism is a dominant force in the world today, and that science has transformed our world. But what if a new mythology could be formed in which spiritual desires are not opposed, but complementary forces? What if our mythology could actually be fully human and holistic?

The Durants see spiritual and religious forces as elemental to binding a society together, creating universal morals, lubricating communication, and laying the foundation for secular progress. When secular forces take power they overreach to cut off the 'ancient' religious ideas. But when spiritual forces are severed from our public life it comes at too great a cost - moral decline, fracture, and decay in a culture. Ultimately mythology is needed to bind us to each other and to a higher morality. We have to learn from and grow from the past, we cannot just move beyond the past blindly and force our spiritual questions down into the collective unconscious. Each of us has to walk through, learn from, and overcome the past, in our own lives individually, and in our society in our collective unconscious. If we honestly confront our past we can learn from it, and we can actually bring matters of the soul into our public discourse. The spiritual can once again become a key part of our collective psyche. We can actually talk about meaning in life, and about the soul.

The Durants spent forty years ruminating on the big questions of history and philosophy. Those big questions are essential. Our view of the modern world has been shaped by this bird's-eye view of history. But ultimately, what they learned for themselves is that, in spite of the big forces at play, we can still each have meaning in our own little world, just as millions of humans who came before us found meaning in creating and shaping their little worlds. I believe it is worth quoting from a couple paragraphs from the Durants, from *The Gentle Philosopher*:

> It is a mistake to think that the past is dead. Nothing that has ever happened is quite without influence at this moment. The present is merely the past rolled up and concentrated in this second of time. You, too, are your past; often your face is your autobiography; you are what you are because of what you have been; because of your heredity stretching back into forgotten generations; because of every element of the environment that has affected you, every man or woman that has met you, every book that you have read, every experience that you have had; all these are accumulated in your memory, your body, your character, your soul. So with a city, a country, and a race; it is its past, and cannot be understood without it.
>
> Perhaps the cause of our contemporary pessimism is our tendency to view history as a turbulent stream of conflicts - between individuals in economic life, between groups in politics, between creeds in religion, between states in war. This is the more dramatic side of history; it captures the eye of the historian and the interest of the reader. But if we turn from that Mississippi of strife, hot with hate and dark with blood, to look upon the banks of the stream, we find quieter but more inspiring scenes: women rearing children, men building homes, peasants drawing food from the soil, artisans making the conveniences of life, statesmen sometimes organizing peace instead of war, teachers forming savages into citizens, musicians taming our hearts with harmony and rhythm, scientists patiently accumulating knowledge, philosophers groping for truth, saints suggesting the wisdom of love. History has been too often a picture of the bloody stream. The history of civilization is a record of what happened on the banks.[13]

On the banks. The Durants show us that if we believe in the soul, then our path springs out of our belief in a daily practical way. Each person 'on the bank' is a world unto themself. Each person on the bank has a soul and should be treated as such. I also have a soul and must treat myself as such, in this moment in time, on the bank. History moves down the river looking like a tremendous glacier to us, it moves so slowly, barely creaking, humongously imposing, we gaze on it with awe. But we are on the bank, washing our clothing and getting ready for bed, doing the things humans do and have always done through all of time. From the view of the glacier we are born, live, struggle, reproduce, and die in the blink of an eye. And so any mythology must be coherent from a bird's-eye view, from the glacier, and from our view, on the bank. Wide angle and zoomed in.

One of the problems of the modern world is digital technology has flattened our view of ourselves and each other, and our mythologies have come colliding together. Religious mythologies used to give people a coherent view of the world, both the divine view and a view of themselves, so the mythology gave them multiple lenses with which to view the world. Without this kind of holistic mythology it is very difficult to see and understand both the gigantic glacier, and the small people on the bank. A lens for both the universe and our own soul. We struggle to see both at once with our limited human capacity.

On the bank our belief is what forms our path. If the path is our movement over time, then our ethics inform the daily steps taken. Our ethical behavior flows out from our belief - that within each person is a soul, a soul capable of transcending the body. Over time our ethics make a path which gives rise to change, growth, and meaning in our soul. Eventually we hope to alter the path of the glacier, but we begin by changing our own soul.

The language of the soul is connected to the body. We feel the impact of a song, or a movie, or a painting, deep within our body. Sometimes we feel we must wall ourselves off from deep emotions, for self-protection, and it seems like we lose the ability to feel them. We don't know what we will find if we descend. That is why it is ultimately an act of courage to silence all distractions, devices, everything that bathes your senses, and be quiet with your own soul. Art shows courage within the struggle, with beauty, and even a glimpse of courage and hope can rescue a drowning soul. And if it speaks to one soul it speaks to many many souls, because souls are fundamentally universal in emotional language.

The language of the soul is connected to the body, but it is not only the body. The body resonates in tune with something deeper within the soul. The deep guttural cry of the sufi musician is a cry out of the soul that resonates at a core level within us. The artist ultimately aims to express that cry, that is to express the cry of the soul through their craft. Transcendent experiences can rock us to the core, transforming our soul, mythologized as a new birth and a new life. Artists are very familiar with this process of self-transformation. So we do already, as artists, acknowledge a soul exists. A soul that can be transformed and made new. We must now make this mythology explicit.

The guiding light for our soul is our mythology. Mythology is the story into which we fit everything we encounter. Mythology tells the story which shows where we've come from and where we are going, from the highest viewpoint possible. It is the lens that puts our lives into context, surrounding our consciousness. This context provides a grounding for our psyche which gives us a firm foundation to unlock its power. Without a mythology we are forever torn between competing views of the world, as each lens would dictate a different set of actions over time. We are tossed about on angry waves and feel helpless.

Consider the story of Apollos. Apollos grew up a poor youth on the streets of Rome. He used to hide outside the workshops of the great sculpture-makers of his day, and eventually a master sculpturist saw him and offered him an apprenticeship. Apollos studied faithfully under his master until he eventually surpassed him by sculpting some of the most beautiful human faces ever put into stone.

Now, by the telling of that story Apollos is a noble hero who overcame great obstacles to create impactful beauty. The mythology helped make that ethical determination. But by another view, the Roman empire was one of the most brutal to have existed, crushing indigenous tribes, sacking cultural artifacts, raping, crucifying local leaders, and then taxing the survivors by force. In the capital of this brutal empire, Apollos spent his whole life chipping on rocks for the wealthy. He is a fool, at best an accessory to evil.

These two views of Apollos conflict directly. Is Apollos a fool or a hero? The lens of mythology helps us understand the context to make these ethical decisions. In the modern world the brain is unmoored from context which creates profound angst. We don't know which lens is right, or good, or true. This is why a coherent mythology is needed. We stand in the middle of a gigantic forest, a thousand paths unfolding in front of us. Art can show the outcome of these paths which helps us understand which path actually has utility for our lives and our present time.

One of the most profound things art can show us is that both views of Apollos are true at the same time, even though they do conflict. It all depends on the level at which you decide to anchor your ethical viewpoint. In other words, your lens. Instead of a debate over which lens is true, the better question is: which lens is the most useful? Which actually brings about harmony and beauty in society? Which brings human community, co-operation, environmental sustainability, and hope? Because with a flawed lens society can suffer tremendously. We stand at a crossroads of history. All knowledge lies before us, accessible to each of us through the newly bestowed power of technology. Which lens we choose will have tremendous ramifications.

The problem of Apollos is a problem of knowledge. From our vantage point we see the progression in full context of history and the world, and we can see the larger ethical dilemma Apollos is born into. If Apollos could see the entirety of the Roman empire's history and future, if Apollos had our lens, what should he have done? Or would this existential knowledge just have paralyzed him entirely? This is the problem with our modern condition, we have come to know too much. Taking away all of that knowledge, we can only reasonably ask Apollos to act as one thrown soul, thrown into a body, into a malnourished family in Rome. To make the most of his place, time, gifts, and vision, as far as he can see.

Each lens produces a path, because each mythology produces a moral foundation that leads to a set of actions over time in the individual. Art makes up the constituent components of the myth and represents it for our collective psyche in a constant feedback loop. Children grow into adolescents, and become sponges for culture and mythology, interacting with it in realtime as they seek to move through the world with success, mediated through corporations. They place their life in context of the myth, and use its framework to decide which path to take. That is why parents so often feel as if they are fighting a losing battle when it comes to culture, it is truly the air we breathe.

A flawed view of the world produces real-life consequences. Stumbling around in the dark, those who walk with a flawed lens end up shipwrecked and broken. What we do flows out of what we believe and what story we are playing a part in. Every thriving society has had strong unifying mythologies that smooth the social fabric. This sense of security and meaning frees up tremendous energy that flows throughout the people as one, creating productivity and harmony. We see it across many societies at various times in history, including ours.

One of the most powerful things art can do is adjust our lens so we view the world more in light of present reality, no matter how painful. Art can do this in both the creator and the receiver. The artist is thus transformed by the act of creating, never to be the same. New routes mapped into the unconscious, new complexity of emotion. It's like giving birth in some ways, as both mother and child are transformed.

Today, it is clear a new mythology is needed, and the groundwork can only be laid with art. For the first time in human history there is the beginning of a global collective mind, both conscious and unconscious. For the first time all human minds and hearts are being connected. A strong mythological foundation will be needed to provide context and truth to this greater collective. This means artists have an extremely difficult challenge that must be approached with a sober mind. The time is short. And unfortunately artists in modern times have not lived up fully to this challenge.

For the last seventy-five years America has been a global creator and exporter of art, culture, and mythology. In America in the 1990s, nihilism, anarchy, despair, and debauchery were dominant youth cultural myths. These unfolded in pathways through time across many lives, all of them unfolding in different ways but with similarly destructive ends. In the 90s, anarchy and nihilism felt like a relief from the hair-metal and synth-pop hyper-optimism of the 80s. Nihilism also felt like a natural outflow of a scientific view of the world at the time. If humans are just biology floating in empty space, there is no soul to commune with and no higher truth to obtain. The quest for meaning became meaningless, so nihilism appeared to be the natural outcome. Music mythologized nihilism - all is meaningless, even the self. There is no real soul, so the self is just a body that can be destroyed. Along with this came increased moral relativism - other people could be used and discarded if it furthered your immediate desires, which led to blatant abuse. If we look there is wreckage everywhere from shipwrecked mythologies.

Hedonism in the 90s was made possible by the collective freeing of minds and bodies in the 60s. The hippie story was born out of a large generation of youth straining against the wartime and corporate mythologies wrestling for power at the time. They correctly diagnosed that culture was repressing human spiritual needs for transcendence and meaning and bodily expression. And over time this quest got simplified into, 'be less repressed and just give in to impulses of the body', culminating in the cocaine binges of the 70s and 80s. By the 90s, those clinging on to this myth to find their highest values were shipwrecked and strung out on drugs. But there was another subset of hippies who went on to find some level of spiritual enlightenment, in both eastern and western forms, following in the ways of George Harrison and Cat Stevens.

It's easy to look back on the hippies as naive but they bravely imagined a different world could exist, and they were pushing outward together for meaning and transcendence. They show that collective effort can create mythology. It has recently happened and it will happen again. They were thrown into the suit-and-tie culture of the 50s and understandably rebelled against it collectively, which then became wrapped up into a new cultural mythology. But the core flaw in the hippie mythology was the glorification of the immediate desires of the self. They continued the human trend of underestimating the downside, in this case the downside of immediately giving in to every momentary desire. The downside is you trade your future self for your present self. And eventually you are your future self, and you sit in brokenness and regret. Your future self lasts much longer than your present self. Your future self lasts the rest of your life. So gratifying immediate desires without restraint brings only pain.

Contrasting the two decades, the 60s correctly diagnosed our need for meaning, belonging, and expression. But the culture underestimated the human condition, the dark side of our nature and needs, which eventually culminated in the mythological Altamonte riots with the Rolling Stones at the end of 1969. The 90s correctly understood the darkness, depravity, and feelings of meaninglessness of the human condition. But the culture left out transcendence, hope, belonging, and growth, which ultimately led to hopelessness, addiction, and degradation. And so now, any new mythology that unfolds must incorporate both the flawed human condition and the need for meaning, hope, transcendence, and expression.

We must use past mythologies with destructive outcomes as our classroom - the study of our past cultural mythologies creates a broad 'lived' mythology for us of what we must avoid. If we let them, they can act as lighthouses while eternally at sea. In this way we can create new myths, intentionally and with intelligence, that will unfold over time with utility. At the very least we can avoid past mistakes, instead of endlessly recycling them in new clothes. The master artist studies both the mythologies of the world and of lives that have come before, absorbs their lessons, ruminates on it all, and makes something new.

In *Merchant, Soldier, Sage* David Priestland discusses the three categories of mythologies that have dominated the western world in various turns.[14] These mythologies arise out of the people who live them, the merchants, priests, and military, and their mythologies vie for dominance with often violent results. When one mythology dominates, the society primarily values the ideals of the myth. According to Priestland the merchant mythology was dominant in western society in modern times until the world wars, when the soldier mythology of bravery and honor took over. This ceded way eventually to the merchant again in the 1970s, which has remained the dominant mythology until the present. And so, consumer mythology lies underneath all of our current mythologies with its highest values of self, wealth, work, status, and material success.

The accumulation of things for the self, manufacturing a curated image of perfection to be displayed. Always working, striving to obtain more things, loaded down with debt. A shallow heart with shallow values, chasing shallow things that we know for certain are meaningless, regretting it on our deathbed. Striving to obtain more than our neighbors, we are forever consuming like locusts until the grass is gone and there is nothing left to eat. We can feel the dissonance with our soul, the skin no longer fits. It feels like a skin it is time to shed.

Most of our modern merchant myths have been built on a foundational cult of youth, the ideal consumer age full of energy and impulse. But a culture built on youth will never have wisdom, always energy but never wisdom. And wisdom will be desperately needed in the years to come. There is nothing inherently wrong with a mythology of youth, the danger is when youth becomes the only mythology. If all the world is viewed through the lens of youth then our elders are weak, without anything to offer. But we know this is false. Most all ancient cultures on earth honor their elders through their mythology. We feel the dissonance between this mythology and our soul, because it's not true or helpful. As the world grows more dangerous and uncertain, the wisdom that our elders bring becomes more and more valuable, and our mythology should reflect that insight. How can our existing mythology move us into the future?

A culture that worships youth exerts pressure on us to try to look forever young, altering our bodies and faces in pursuit of a goal that can never be reached as our bodies endlessly betray us and only grow older. Tremendous suffering has been inflicted because of this mythology on so many people over time, and it is false and wrong. It exerts endless pressure on the young, and corporations leverage the cultural insecurity with an unbelievable inhumanity. And now this myth has been amplified millions of times over by digital technology and the message is the same: your visual appearance is what drives your worth as a person. This cult is cruel and an impossible master to please. And yet we amplify, or simply ignore it. All the while it is literally the air we breathe, changing us over time.

Similarly, a sole mythology erected around technological optimism could become disconnected from primal human emotions, especially negative ones, which are repressed into the collective unconscious and then can re-emerge violently. The mythologies of the merchants have merged with mythologies of technological optimism, and produced success beyond our wildest dreams. Our ability has outrun our mythology. A small number of technology corporations are close to owning most of the world, because they played the capitalistic mythology out too well. And now even they don't know what to do with this unprecedented power, because the capitalistic mythology doesn't show us what to do when you win the game. It's clear that we need a new holistic mythology that incorporates all of life and provides light that guides us morally.

American myths have elevated the self over the collective, the unashamed worship of self: power, fame, wealth, and identity. The self-sufficient cowboy and the self-serving seeker of pleasure and fame. America spun this myth from gold, connected the globe digitally, and then exported these myths to the world, who imbibed them with more or less reservation. The world became drunk on self. Money flowed into these hubs of culture. But over time these myths have hollowed out our souls and left us lonely and depressed, desperate for connection and meaning. In my view these myths did not flow out of any evil human intention but were rather the natural outflow of our unconscious - our immediate, primal, human desires for youth, wealth, sex, and status.

But now our eyes have been forced open. We see now that these myths are only selfish, not wise or useful. These selfish mythologies combined with our primal selfish impulses with a kind of unholy synergy. And now we are watching dragons emerge from the abyss, dragons of our creation, born of our own mythologies. And now we can see the wreckage left behind. So finally, if these myths are no longer useful, they must subside and give way to new myths that have utility to bring about actual human fulfilment and community. A myth that is no longer useful must give way. Mythology that causes destruction must be countered and shown to be empty. Shown for what it is, exposed, and cast away.

Culture accumulates onto itself over time, the glacier in the river, so slowly that we barely notice it as humans. But one thing history shows is that culture progresses, usually in the direction of the highest values of its mythology. Thin layerings of culture are deposited over time, and within a few generations the culture is in a new place.

In many ancient societies there was a mythology that a deceased ones' soul carried on into the afterlife at the point of burial. Tangled up and affiliated with this belief was the sub-belief that the items which were buried with the body would be there in the underworld. Initially this was likely simple trinkets, for example a favorite necklace, or favorite articles of clothing. But the wealthy decided if this was really true, then the way to a successful afterlife was to fill your tomb with supplies and wealth. Maybe the priestly class initially tried to reign this in unsuccessfully. Over time the ruling class of some societies were buried with chariots, drinking cauldrons, jewels and gold of all kinds, along with even servants, wives and animals. Some societies are believed to have literally buried themselves into poverty, because so much wealth was interned with the elite, in the sacred ground never to come back out (or at least until a millennia or two later). The mythology appeared normal and harmless, but over time the society moved more and more towards its highest values, until it became destructive. This is really the human story if you study history at all. Western society had dueling as a normal means of settling disagreements well into the 1800s, which is unimaginable to us today.

What this shows us is that mythologies that were once good can turn bad. A better way of stating that might be a mythology which once was quite useful can lose its utility. A mythology of youth might have been very useful at one time for a country trying to get onto its economic feet after war, but over time it can become destructive. It turns into a visually obsessed youth culture, trying to curate an online story for the world, altering their bodies while hating themselves, knowing all the while the planet is being overconsumed. Sociologists have known that our conspicuously consuming culture was bad for us, and that trying to search for meaning by putting on a show for our neighbors is the worst kind of life. But instead of listening to our elders and teachers we fell into our primal impulses, and magnified this effect into a gigantic digital infrastructure, so that performing for your neighbors became almost pathological.

A mythology of genius might have cultivated original artists but it also led to blatant abuse by people in power. A mythology of wealth and consumption might have seemed fun and harmless in the 80s, during Baywatch and daytrading, but when so many people are suffering it can feel inhumanly vapid and shallow. And the hiphop stars and other few lucky ones will consume, consume, consume, conspicuously on stage, while the poor of the world watch, and while the actual planet is the thing consumed. There will undoubtedly be a totally different planet for future generations, and if our mythologies don't alter how can we even hope to carry on?

If we imagine our culture as a tremendously large organism, diffuse, like the fungus that covers over two thousand acres in Malheur Forest in Oregon. One diffuse organism. Mythology is like the skin the organism wears and maneuvers in and generally takes for granted. The culture has rapidly expanded to include the whole digitally connected world, so the organism has grown humongous and the skin no longer fits. Right now, the organism is sick and shuddering and the skin has grown necrotic. A metamorphosis of mythology must occur, like the cicada, the organism struggling out of its skin to become something new. It's a painful struggle, but when the time comes there is no other choice. The cicada moves on, and a translucent shell of skin will be left behind on the tree. Now is the time for artists, because the merchants have lost moral leadership and the soldiers are sidelined. Artists have the only solution to the problem. To put it quite directly, artists are the new sages, and the sages must now lead.

Artists are the new sages, the new priests. I say this simply as an acknowledgement of present reality, not to be blasphemous in any way. The artist strives to express the inexpressible, the 'ineffable'. A profound work of art expresses things we cannot speak, but which are deeply true. This used to be the role of the sage/shaman/priest. Western society has forgotten there are many essential things in life that cannot be expressed through language. In the new digital age, everything is mediated through language, but what if this bottleneck causes us to lose something profound, deeper truths that live beyond language?

What would be the characteristics of a new mythology? A very difficult question, because as humans we are always stuck within our current mythology and can't even properly envision anything else. One possible answer comes from someone who thought quite a bit about this subject, Austrian psychiatrist Victor Frankl. Frankl was a practicing psychiatrist during the Nazi takeover of Austria, and he had studied both suicide and depression in Vienna. Because he was of Jewish descent he eventually lost much of his practice and ended up imprisoned in various concentration camps for several months. His thoughts and observations while in Nazi concentration camps would become his book *Man's Search for Meaning* published in 1946.

While in the concentration camps he meditated on suffering - how suffering was a fundamental component of life, and if suffering is fundamental, then in order to pass through suffering successfully our mythology must be greater than just status and possessions. When there is no circumstantial happiness, or even hope for happiness, there still can be meaning, and Frankl observed those who had a strong core of meaning brave the camps for the most part emotionally and spiritually intact, even if they didn't ultimately survive. He also saw many others who seemed to give in to death, and he attributed their dying to a loss of will to live, as after much suffering some prisoners would simply give up, stop working, smoke a cigarette, and wait to be put to death by the guards.

But Frankl astutely observed that what he was watching in the camps was just the experience of every individual in the world, writ small, and sped up. Everyone will suffer and die, and those that find meaning are able to transcend the self, so that even in suffering there is meaning. He described a moment he found meaning thinking of his wife who would soon be put to death, in the prison camp,

> Another time we were at work in a trench. The dawn was grey around us; grey was the sky above; grey the snow in the pale light of dawn; grey the rags in which my fellow prisoners were clad, and grey their faces. I was again conversing silently with my wife, or perhaps I was struggling to find the *reason* for my sufferings, my slow dying. In a last violent protest against the hopelessness of imminent death, I sensed my spirit piercing through the enveloping gloom. I felt it transcend that hopeless, meaningless world, and from somewhere I heard a victorious "Yes" in answer to my question of the existence of an ultimate purpose. At that moment a light was lit in a distant farmhouse, which stood on the horizon as if painted there, in the midst of the miserable grey of a dawning morning in Bavaria. "Et lux in tenebris lucet" - and the light shineth in the darkness. For hours I stood hacking at the icy ground. The guard passed by, insulting me, and once again I communed with my beloved. More and more I felt that she was present, that she was with me; I had the feeling that I was able to touch her, able to stretch out my hand and grasp hers. The feeling was very strong: she was there. Then, at that very moment, a bird flew down silently and perched just in front of me, on the heap of soil which I had dug up from the ditch, and looked steadily at me.[15]

Frankl found a moment of transcendence in a brutal world, and that brought a sense of meaning that was outside of himself. The sense of meaning was brought about by meditating on his wife, even though she was not there. Frankl went on to use these experiences to develop a psychotherapeutic school of thought centered on 'logotherapy', which primarily aimed at helping patients find meaning. Logotherapy was a system in which the psychotherapist seeks to help the patient unveil the real sources of meaning in their own life that they should be pursuing.

Frankl's book is quite useful because it doesn't attempt to analyze as much as it simply tells the story and observes both the struggle and absurdity. After thought and contemplation, Frankl left the camps with the observation that meaning can be found through three sources, all of which achieve some level of transcendence of self:

1. *Experience* - A transcendent experience with someone or something. Frankl found this by communing with his wife in his mind in the middle of the lowest point of his life, and this is the transcendent potential of love. This could also come about by a profound encounter with some thing, like a beautiful work of art, or an enveloping sunset, or towering mountains, or looking down from outer space.

2. *Creation/work* - Frankl's drive to survive was supplemented by his burning desire to get his book manuscript out of the camp. It was his quest and he felt he had made a fundamental discovery about human nature that could change the world. He wrote pieces of it on bits of paper lying around the camp. He felt consumed by a desire to accomplish his task and communicate the wisdom he had discovered, and meaning arose out of this quest. So meaning arises in creation of art, a pouring out of the soul, or to some degree in any kind of work that expresses its creator.

3. *Suffering* - Suffering is the means of last resort. If love and creative work haven't brought transcendence of self then suffering will, in the end, do its work. Frankl saw depression as the result of too large a gap between your potential and reality, your dreams and your situation. This triggers existential angst which Frankl sees as a blessing, forcing us to face our mortality and exercise risks for freedom to overcome our suffering. Enduring suffering bravely produced meaning to Frankl, "By accepting the challenge to suffer bravely, life has a meaning up to the last moment."

Frankl helps to tune our mythology to the right tone - our mythology must address the basic human experience of suffering, and the basic human need for meaning. Frankl found that meaning comes from pouring yourself out in art, in work, in love, and in suffering. This is the opposite of a mythology of self-worship. It means finding meaning for yourself begins with getting outside of yourself. The path to meaning is what Irish philosopher Iris Murdoch called 'to unself'.[16]

Unselfing is deeply connected with the fact that every human being has a basic drive to create. We can think of this as the impression of unselfing, as one unselfs one moves towards creating, or pours oneself out in creation. This drive to create moves in us to create offspring, to create families, to create communities, to create work, to create art, to create music, to create life. To create harmony out of chaos by unselfing. To push out with the self into nothingness. We encounter resistance but we push on outwards and create, this is the fundamental drive of life. Imagine a mythology that represented each human as a creative soul, a source of creativity meant to live up to imbued potential. Within you is a unique new branch of the creative tree, waiting to be unfolded, green with life inside the trunk. It can only come from you and it is utterly unique. And thus each of us are unselfed in creation.

To think more about unselfing, consider two performers in the same play. One of them is a primary character, onstage the majority of the play, and when she is out on stage it is a transcendent feeling. She becomes literally 'lost in the moment' of the play. The other actor has a small role, just a few chorus lines, but when out on stage she becomes lost in the moment with the same transcendent feeling. If they both are similar in psyche, which is likely to receive a greater feeling of meaning from the play?

I would argue the greater meaning would likely be with the one who was the most poured out, onstage every moment, pushed to the edges of her skill level in front of the audience. She is the most unselfed, and receives the most meaning, all other things being equal. So it is my observation that being unselfed is a process, and meaning increases the further unselfed we become. It is the same feeling that comes over a master carpenter who becomes lost in the craft - complete unselfing can bring that deeper level of meaning. Or a violinist soloing with intense passion. Or a pair of lovers on a walk, who suddenly become lost in each other's eyes. They are unselfed in the moment, and meaning arises. Or a mother breastfeeding her newborn. Similarly, consider parents at their child's college graduation, overflowing with pride and joy. An uncle attending that same graduation, although happy for the child, can never obtain the same depth of meaning because his life was not unselfed for that child in the same way as the parents.

And here is the great irony of the American dream - does the 'pursuit of happiness' point us in the wrong direction? It looks as if happiness appears when one is pouring out oneself, unselfing, which is quite different than making happiness itself the pursuit. If the pursuit of happiness is the wrong story then we need to extricate ourselves from the story.

John Stuart Mill was a British economist and philosopher who championed liberty and free markets. He was a founder of Utilitarianism, which held that society should be structured to achieve the greatest happiness for the most individuals. In his *Autobiography of J.S.Mill* he recounts how, in the winter of 1826-27, he fell into a deep depression. Suicidal, he immersed himself in the beauty of nature and poetry, and slowly emerged with the following epiphany,

> I never, indeed, wavered in the conviction that happiness is the test of all rules of conduct, and the end of life. But I now thought that this end was only to be attained by not making it the direct end. Those only are happy (I thought) who have their minds fixed on some object other than their own happiness; on the happiness of others, on the improvement of mankind, even on some art or pursuit, followed not as a means, but as itself an ideal end. Aiming thus at something else, they find happiness by the way. The enjoyments of life (such was now my theory) are sufficient to make it a pleasant thing, when they are taken en passant, without being made a principal object. Once make them so, and they are immediately felt to be insufficient. They will not bear a scrutinizing examination. Ask yourself whether you are happy, and you cease

> to be so. The only chance is to treat, not happiness, but some end external to it, as the purpose of life. Let your self-consciousness, your scrutiny, your self-interrogation, exhaust themselves on that; and if otherwise fortunately circumstanced you will inhale happiness with the air you breathe, without dwelling on it or thinking about it, without either forestalling it in imagination, or putting it to flight by fatal questioning. This theory now became the basis of my philosophy of life. And I still hold to it as the best theory for all those who have but a moderate degree of sensibility and of capacity for enjoyment, that is, for the great majority of mankind.[17]

The realization of John Stuart Mill is the same realization that has begun to dawn on all modern people - that happiness cannot be obtained by making it your sole goal. That one must aim at something greater than oneself, and then meaning can at times appear through unselfing. Why do we have to wait until each of us has had this epiphany to actually create something new?

Abraham Maslow was an American psychologist of Jewish descent whose parents emigrated from Kiev in the early 1900s, and he approached psychology from a very different perspective than Freud. Freud viewed psychology as fundamentally about deficiencies in meeting our needs, and ultimately he saw all human needs as being grounded in the sexual. Freud was a towering figure and tremendously influential, but also rigid and controlling, and eventually some of his followers, like Carl Jung and Otto Rank, broke away from him over this view of the human psyche.

Where Freud viewed the human mind through the lens of a doctor seeking to cure the sick, Jung viewed the mind as a mysterious source of symbolism we can learn to understand and navigate, the accumulation of our primal unconscious. Jung and Rank saw spiritual drives and artistic symbolism as being fundamental to what it means to be human, even potentially greater than sexual drives, and they postulated that a higher state of ideal being was available to humans.

Maslow took these ideas and expanded on them in his book *Motivation and Personality* in 1954, and along with Carl Rogers founded 'positive psychology', a branch of psychology that sought to uncover how humans could live the most fulfilled life, instead of focusing on only overcoming deficiencies. Maslow is famous for his 'hierarchy of needs', but later in life he spent much of his time studying what he called 'self-actualized' people, people who appeared to have arrived at a fulfilled state of being, living a life of meaning.

He observed that many of these self-actualized people had encountered what he called 'peak experiences', moments of transcendence in their life that changed the way they viewed the world. Some of the characteristics of a peak experience include the loss of judgement for time and space, the feeling of being a part of a harmonious whole, as well as a feeling of warmth and complete absorption in the moment. As he described it in his later book *The Farther Reaches of Human Nature*,

> Peak experiences are transient moments of self-actualization. They are moments of ecstasy which cannot be bought, cannot be guaranteed, cannot even be sought. One must be, as C.S. Lewis wrote, "surprised by joy." But one can set up the conditions so that peak experiences are more likely, or one can perversely set up the conditions so that they are less likely. Breaking up an illusion, getting rid of a false notion, learning what one is not good at, learning what one's potentialities are not - these are also part of discovering what one is in fact.[18]

Going into this transcendent world even one time was very impactful for the people in Maslow's studies. Through his studies and interviews, Maslow came to see this as a universal state of being that all humans have access to, and he called it 'being-cognition', or B-cognition. According to Maslow B-cognition is a lens through which we view the world as one single whole. We are fully present, and a part of the present moment, which we are working to mold and shape. It's very similar in concept to mindfulness, or practicing presence, with an emphasis on transcendence of self.

Maslow found that this B-cognition lens views the world through certain values, which appear for the most part to be the universal values of artists, prophets, poets, and mystics. The values of transcendence. If these values ring out in your soul, then here is a signpost on our quest for a mythology, because these appear to be universal:

Truth, Goodness, Beauty, Wholeness, Aliveness, Uniqueness, Perfection, Completion, Justice, Simplicity, Richness, Effortlessness, Playfulness, and *Self-Sufficiency.*

To look at a few:

Truth

If you look at artists throughout history their primary aim is towards full truth. Anything that detracts from truth needs to be discarded. Nothing false can be communicated when fully in this state of being. The history of art shows a drive towards greater truth. Art is especially adept at exposing hypocrisy, which artists hate.

The true life is the life fully aligned with the reality around it as it is known and experienced. Full reality, unashamed and unafraid. Truth can be painful but is always useful. A life lived within the framework of a lie is no life at all - it may be calm for the time being, but ultimately the truth is better sooner than later. The truth is better now. We are all in Plato's allegory of the cave, looking at shadows on the wall, trying to divine which are real. With digital technology we can use knowledge to see a little farther, if we know how.

Goodness

The artist is oriented towards goodness wherever possible. Giving over taking, kindness over cruelty, unself over self. These all subjugate ultimately to truth, but even the driver for truth is out of goodness and for good to triumph. The prophet calls for repentance and a turn back to goodness. The artist reaches high to illustrate ultimate goodness, but also acknowledges that ultimate good can never be perfectly obtained. That is the nature of the human condition. As moral philosopher Iris Murdoch put it,

"Good lives as it were on both sides of the barrier."[19]

Beauty

Divinely superfluous, beauty reflects the soul's ideal of perfection. The soul when fully expressed uses craft to create beauty with complexity. Beauty pulls us into sudden B-Cognition, into the present moment. We are pulled into the present moment of a sunrise, or the center of a flower, or a shot in a film, or a string quartet.

We turn again to Iris Murdoch, who was a fierce defender of the transcendent power of beauty. She described the effect of beauty eloquently,

> Beauty is the convenient and traditional name of something which art and nature share, and which gives a fairly clear sense to the idea of quality of experience and change of consciousness. I am looking out of my window in an anxious and resentful state of mind, oblivious of my surroundings, brooding perhaps on some damage done to my prestige. Then suddenly I observe a hovering kestrel. In a moment everything is altered. The brooding self with its hurt vanity has disappeared. There is nothing now but kestrel.[19]

Wholeness

Integration of the complete self. The master artist has explored the inner self and navigated the inner divides with some level of clarity. The artist gains some understanding of their own emotions and disparate desires and becomes more whole. Bringing what is hidden out into the light to make it whole, no partial truths and no distortions of view.

Digital technology has brought everything together, all lenses, under one simultaneous spotlight. Immediately our worldviews began to fracture, because as humans we often hold competing views of the world in our minds at the same time. Those who valued greed saw greed played out to the endgame, and realized it wasn't really what they valued at all. Maybe they actually valued goodness instead. This is the feeling of idols tumbling to the ground everywhere. But in a way it can be helpful, a 'dark grace', to see false idols crumble. And now a new lens is needed, a holistic view of ourselves and our place in the world.

Aliveness

Art arises with living energy, this is part of its beauty. Aliveness rooted in the biology of the human body, we experience and create art with aliveness out of every human cell. Just look at anything made by hand - for example clay animation, which feels like a full concentration of the energy that makes the human alive. Alive like a child, with the mind of a child. Art mimics nature in that it feels alive in every part. As the Persian poet Rumi said, "When you do things from your soul you feel a river moving in you, a joy."[20]

Playfulness

Within the creative flow the artist actually does play, and this is fun. Real fun. Playfulness is a common characteristic of an artist in the flow, the rational controlling mind relaxes and the inner child is embodied to play. This feeling of being a child again is the ultimate reward for the master artist - playing like a child but with masterful artistic power, the artist is in a way reborn. It's an addicting feeling, a deeply satisfying feeling. It's a feeling the artist craves. Play is the primary method of discovery - trying out ideas and pushing the boundaries of the art to create something new.

This means that within these peak experiences, values could emerge that were not the original values of the individual. Some would say these are the true desired values of most people when down at the level of the heart

- truth, beauty, justice, wholeness, goodness. We could call these values the collective ideal. The soul, like a child, fundamentally has a heart for what is good and true and whole. Just looking at ourselves from the outside in, we see something deeply universal, which drives art, which contains things that cannot be expressed in language. If we dig very deep there are universal drives toward universal values. Things that are ineffable, deeper than language and culture.

Nature has been delivering peak experiences to humankind for all of history, through sublime beauty and awesome displays of power. Were primal humans always in this transcendent moment? John Muir was a modern mystic, a Scottish poet, philosopher, and naturalist. When he was 28 years old he injured his eyes in a work accident and was blinded for six weeks, which led to an epiphany that he should leave the factories and study the natural world. He eventually fell in love with what would become Yosemite, and was instrumental in establishing the first US national park. As he wrote in his book *The Yosemite* from 1912, "Everybody needs beauty as well as bread, places to play in and pray in, where nature may heal and give strength to body and soul alike."[21] In a 2017 study "Awe, the Small Self, and Prosocial Behavior", scientists from the University of California elicited awe by having subjects gaze up into a huge grove of eucalyptus trees for one minute, with the light filtering through - the awe-inspiring beauty of nature. They found that using nature to experimentally induce awe caused individuals to endorse more ethical decisions, to be more generous to a stranger, and to report more pro-social value as if they felt more part of a collective.[22] Could this awe of nature just be unveiling the soul, the B-cognition that lies beneath? Nature can have that kind of profound power. As American poet Ralph Waldo Emerson described it in his essay *Nature* from 1836,

> In the woods, we return to reason and faith. There I feel that nothing can befall me in life - no disgrace, no calamity (leaving me my eyes), which nature cannot repair. Standing on the bare ground, - my head bathed by the blithe air and uplifted into infinite space - all mean egotism vanishes. I become a transparent eyeball. I am nothing. I see all.[23]

The values that Maslow uncovered are generally in line with the principal values of the major religions, as well as most ethical systems of living. And so we have a religious and psychological basis, and a supremely human basis, for the values of a core mythology. One that doesn't fight our essential humanity. One that acknowledges the soul in each human. One that acknowledges our relationship with and obligation to nature. Flawed, but capable of transcendence. Born to an aging body but capable of transcending it.

Maslow observed self-actualized people driving towards these values. People who live in and are able to work within those values are the 'self-actualized' people. In other words, they have fulfilled those needs. With his non-actualized patients, Maslow began to see this same pattern, the same needs and desires, except they were not being fulfilled. The desire to be a person of truth, beauty, wholeness, and goodness through and through is the human desire, and his patients were frustrated and not able to fulfill these needs and find meaning. And similarly, in our lives in modern culture we experience this dissonance, desires that are not expressed and constantly being frustrated within us, as Maslow said,

> These intrinsic values are instinctoid in nature, i.e., they are needed (a) to avoid illness and (b) to achieve fullest humanness or growth. The "illnesses" resulting from deprivation of intrinsic values (metaneeds) we may call metapathologies. The "highest" values; the spiritual life; the highest aspirations of mankind are therefore proper subjects for scientific study and research. They are in the world of nature.
>
> These metaneeds, though having certain special characteristics which differentiate them from basic needs, are yet in the same realm of discourse of and research as, for instance, the need for Vitamin C or for Calcium.[18]

Maslow also had a warning - if each human has basic drives for these higher values, deep in their soul, then when these desires are frustrated in a society they can pathologize, or turn destructive. In *The Farther Reaches of Human Nature*, Maslow put together a table on these pathologies, and it rings out as an accurate diagnosis of the modern condition:

B-Values	Pathogenic Deprivation	Specific Metapathologies
Truth	Dishonesty	**Mistrust; cynicism; skepticism; suspicion**
Beauty	Ugliness	**Vulgarity; Fatigue; Bleakness**
Aliveness	Deadness. Mechanizing of life.	**Robotizing. Loss of emotion. Feeling oneself to be totally determined.**
Wholeness	Chaos. Atomism.	**Disintegration; "The world is falling apart"**
Simplicity	Confusing Complexity; Disconnectedness	**Overcomplexity; Bewilderment**

If we acknowledge that these are the social pathologies we are now observing in modern countries, then we should look carefully at Maslow's B-Values. If we open our eyes and acknowledge that we are seeing bleakness, robotizing, bewilderment, disintegration, mistrust, and suspicion, then this theory is important to us right now and it is important we take heed. Sometimes certain prophets live and die and their prophecies are not fulfilled until much later. Maslow died almost 50 years ago but it feels like his prophecies have come full circle in relevance. He stands like a lighthouse in an angry ocean.

If these desires/values are truly universal, then we must address them in our mythologies, in our art, in our stories, in our everyday culture, and not repress them into the unconscious. They must become explicit. A mythology whose highest values are wealth, sex, identity, work, youth, commerce, and fame, and worships gratification of immediate desires, will feel forever lacking, and we will feel as if we are forever searching. But Maslow suggests something deeper, which is that frustration can build upon frustration in a society and eventually emerge with great destruction.

A culture is always moving, driving towards a direction, because the youth are always looking to push out towards the highest values. So if we are layering on, layering on, after many layers then where will we be? We are all searchers, searchers of meaning, but what path are we on now? And if technology allows culture to accumulate very rapidly, where are we rapidly heading?

TOWARDS A NEW ETHIC

Mythologies are our lenses for viewing the world, grounded in and formed by art over time. Since it is going to be impossible for this book alone to define a new mythology out of whole cloth, a useful question could be, what would a life lived by this new mythology look like? A more useful phrasing of that question might be, how would this mythology unfold in life over time? What would the path look like? This question gets at the practical meat of it, which is the ethics.

The first thing we could look at is how should we view the world, in light of a new mythology formed around higher values, meaning, and transcendence? Through our new mythological lens we would view ourselves as travelers, a soul thrown both into the world and onto a journey. We would view each person we intersect with as a traveler, so we would see thousands of intertwining paths unfolding over time. Each traveler is a unique world unto themselves, a soul and a will, who has encountered joys, difficulties, and sufferings on their journey. So we cannot judge another person unless we can see their winding path, through sickness, joy, and struggle, trying to maximize their potential in the world. They began as another soul, thrown onto a journey they didn't ask for. We see them only for a moment in time when our paths intersect, but they are also travelers with a long path behind them trying to maximize their potential. Travelers on the bank.

A useful analogy here would be to think of an oak tree seedling, growing up by the side of the road. It didn't ask to be planted there, by the side of the road in sandy soil, catching billows of car emissions, in a time in history when trees are undervalued. It simply arose where it was planted, because it rained, and it is self-evident that its highest aim as a tree is to maximize its potential by growing high and strong, providing homes for birds and shade for animals, dropping leaves and cycling nutrients in the ecosystem, and making acorns that will be dropped by roadsides near and far.

Looking at the oak seedling can help us to answer Apollos' question of ethics. Apollos did not choose to be born at the height of the Roman empire, to a poor family with little resources. He did not choose his birth, upbringing, natural talents, or creative inclinations. So the question of what Apollos should do with his life hinges on thinking about the steps of his path as it unfolds over time. When we think about the life of Apollos, it becomes clear that his only ethical obligation is to walk his journey the best that he can, to maximize his meaning and potential by creating and giving and helping others maximize theirs.

Forces much larger than Apollos were at play during his time, as the common peoples of the Roman world were tossed about on the waves of great empires. And so we look at Apollos and see that each person can only begin to choose from the starting point they are given, with the materials they have to work with. Those are the only options, and the choice, the path, unfolds from there. Each person is, in a sense, a prisoner of wherever they have been thrown. Ethically, we must arise like the young oak tree, accept our cards, and play our hand as best we can. In spite of our thrown-ness, we can overcome, thrive, and effect change. Our obligation is to realize our full oak tree potential.

How would we find our full potential? Here we come to the ethical advice given by student of mythology Joseph Campbell – "follow your bliss."[24] Joseph Campbell advised that travelers on this journey of life seek to find those things that give them joy, transcendence, and a sense of meaning. In popular culture this was translated into, "do what makes you happy." But what Campbell meant is that when you encounter a rare moment of bliss and transcendence, you catch a glimpse of the unfolding of your soul in time. In other words, you were thrown into your soul, but you don't know it well yet. So you must carefully observe it to understand it. As you journey, you should look for those things in life that stir up these emotions of bliss in you and follow those paths into the dark woods. Those moments that resonate in your soul are welcome signposts along the journey. Stop, value them, take heed, and consider your path.

Campbell's advice still is not complete, it is somewhat myopic with a focus only on the self - I don't believe he meant it to exist by itself. So we can amend Campbell's advice with Murdoch, Maslow, and Frankl's observations - that the ultimate path to meaning is through unselfing, pouring out of the self in love, life, creativity, work, family, and sometimes suffering. To merge these concepts succinctly - follow your bliss to create through unselfing. Each traveler is on a journey, seeking to realize their potential and follow their creative bliss, through suffering and difficulty, ultimately finding meaning through their own unselfing.

Following our bliss, realizing our soul's potential, is not unlimited. It is hemmed in by our need to intersect with our fellow travelers, and ultimately help them maximize their own potential soul. We cannot be always bending the wills of others towards our own in unending selfishness. Their path, their journey, is just as much a world of struggle and pain as ours, a world we can't fully know. So we must interact with each traveler with grace, honoring their path. Realization of our potential is also hemmed in by the imperfect world we were thrown into. It will likely never be fully realized, which can cause much frustration and dissonance in our soul. But in the end it is merely a path to follow instead of a destination, and we won't ever arrive. Occasionally, when it appears among us, bliss is like a sign, 'meaning is this way', on the road of life. When we come across that sign we should take note, and look for unfolding paths in that direction.

Is this the right way to see the world? It's not possible for us to even know. We cannot fathom all of the world at once. Instead of right and wrong, we can say this is a true way to see the world. This way lives in harmony with humanity, in harmony with nature, in harmony with ourselves.

Imagine two travelers that end up on the same road together. They are both traveling by the north star. One of them points to a bright star far in the distance and says, "that is the north star that has guided me." The other says, "No, the star beside is the north star, I am certain." They argue and eventually part ways. But what they fail to see is that they both are headed the same exact direction, no matter which of them was correct. Following either star would unfold in the same path. So why not cooperate together, support each other, and produce synergy? And that is how I believe we can come to a universal ethic - a path we can all walk on together, even if following different north stars.

As we travel, our values should not be status, wealth, sex, or fame. They must be the highest values, of artists and poets and prophets, those ultimate values that cause the least dissonance in our soul. Truth, beauty, goodness, wholeness, aliveness. And so we must only speak truth to each other and to ourselves. And hold ourselves to what we know is true. Listen to the dissonance between our higher values and our actions, our culture, our words, our art, and move towards harmony. To quote Will Durant again, "We are what we repeatedly do. Excellence, then, is not an act but a habit."[25]

We should look for opportunities to pour out ourself in love, and give fully to another. Or to pour out ourself in creation, and seek to master our craft. We must be open to a sudden pouring in - of nature, or of art, or of music; we must be open to those transcendent moments. And then ultimately we pour out ourself in suffering, by walking through our suffering with bravery over our fear.

Walking with bravery is our best ethic, our best path to becoming our full selves. Nietzsche described it beautifully,

> No one can build you the bridge on which you, and only you, must cross the river of life. There may be countless trails and bridges and demigods who would gladly carry you across; but only at the price of pawning and forgoing yourself. There is one path in the world that none can walk but you. Where does it lead? Don't ask, walk![26]

As artists we must walk our own (sometimes lonely) path and, as Polish sculpturist Stanis Szukalski said, suck our world out of our own thumbs.[27] Because no one else can unfold our own soul for us, this is our path to walk and unfold. But it is also a quest, because you truly do not know what you will uncover about your soul as you begin to unfold it. You are the only one who has that particular soul. Each person has a world to learn about themself, more than many lifetimes can unfold. Our obligation is to be honest with ourselves and true to our soul.

e.e. cummings was an American modern poet who loved playing with words and hated capitalization and authority. He was entirely himself, and was always struggling with traditionalists who did not like his freeform way of expression. He put it this way, in a letter to a high school newspaper editor who asked him for advice on how to become a poet,

> To be nobody-but-yourself - in a world which is doing its best, night and day, to make you everybody else - means to fight the hardest battle which any human being can fight; and never stop fighting.
>
> And so my advice to all young people who wish to become poets is: do something easy, like learning how to blow up the world - unless you're not only willing, but glad, to feel and work and fight till you die.
>
> Does that sound dismal? It isn't.
> t's the most wonderful life on earth.
> Or so I feel.[28]

cummings put it quite well. It may well be difficult to forge a path for our soul, but there is no real alternative. This is our lot as an oak seedling, to pick up where we have been thrown and begin to emerge, reaching upward for the light and downwards for the soil. Like the young oak stretching out towards the sun, we can only become more or less of an oak tree, and reach more of less of our potential. Similarly a hemp seedling, given the right soil and amendments and water, will push outward and become a giant plant, full of leaves and flowers for fiber and oil. It naturally reaches out for its full potential if the conditions allow. In the same way, a baby in the womb stretches and grows and continues to open outward as the child shows its own personality over time, unfolding its own soul, its own struggle.

Through the struggle we pour out ourself, and ultimately in suffering we grow and are transformed and eventually we seek to overcome suffering with dignity. A caterpillar stretches and grows, and then cocoons, without ever having a glimpse of itself as a butterfly until the moment arrives, but it reaches nonetheless towards its ultimate potential. So we cannot know what we will become or where the path will lead but we unfold. Ultimately we can ask, what kind of person would this mythology create? An integrated person, only speaking truth, with openness, empathy, and integrity, and an aliveness of spirit.

As artists we have a difficult challenge in front of us. Those who came before have shipwrecked and now we stand on the bow. There are no good mythologies left standing, no real collective ones for a new humanity, so the time is short. The artist faces into the wind with eyes wide open, seeing what is true and real and what approaches appears to be darkened. Mythology must guide us with its light, and leaders must not be afraid to use the light. The artist is the sage who must now speak what is true with confidence.

Each particular artist must now illuminate because a collective explosion of light is needed within this present time. Right now on this path in this world in our story. The time is now and the urgency is real. Only an explosion of truth from the soul can light the way right now. Humans can do this, we have done it before. Art can light the way, unfolding like a footlamp for the soul. That story must be embodied now.

THE TWO KNOWLEDGES

The pathway of the artist can be arduous and tortured. Art must be incubated before it is embodied and created. Wisdom accumulates, experience deepens. Along the path there are two areas of knowledge we must focus our attention on in the day to day: the knowledge of the self, and the knowledge of the craft.

Knowledge of the craft can dazzle at first, but if it is divorced from the soul's creative fire it rings hollow. Excellence of craft requires discipline of the mind and body, and so we admire it wherever it is found. But mastery of craft is only a prerequisite to mastery of the whole art. Total mastery, which can never be fully achieved, would be perfection of craft in service to clarity of soul.

We master our craft in order to have it at the ready for the unconscious to act upon. Our mastery will determine the ceiling of our emotional expression from a technical standpoint. An artist who is not disciplined will be limited in their craft by their ability to express complex emotion. They will also be limited in their ability to express originality on command through craft, and that is often a prerequisite to enter the realm of making truly transcendent artwork.

The work of a master artist is unmistakable because of its originality - no one else could have created it, in no other place and time. It stands utterly unique, because it represents a unique soul unfolded in time. This kind of mastery of the craft involves the whole body, as we learn to express deeper and more complex emotion, on impulse from the unconscious. At this level both the ego of the self and the skill of the craft become transparent.

As American painter Andrew Wyeth said, "I want to paint a picture with nothing but a soul."[29]

Mastery of craft requires self-discipline. Knowledge of the self requires an open flexibility of mind. Both of these are rarely found in the same person. One might be a savant expressionist digging deep into the psyche, the other commands a honed skillset that can create complex craft on command. Sometimes these do come together and the results are transformational - when the deep thinker masters a craft, or when a skilled craftsman has a transcendent experience. This combining of powers is the master artist's ultimate toolset. The artist must understand how and when to combine craft with emotion, in synergy together and shading each other in contrast, at the highest level of the craft.

Study any of the great thinkers, philosophers, mystics, and you will find one common thread: they all refer to mastery of the will over the body. The body communicates to the will but is in submission. Think of the first time you realized you could feel an emotion and not act on it - that was a powerful self-realization. A split opened up in your psyche, a useful split. Emotions, and the body, are able to be brought under control of the will.

To further provoke this split between body and will, some mystics will set out on a quest, a part of which involves some kind of painful mortification of the body. Subjugation through trial, pain, and endurance. Walking up thousands of steps barefoot, flagellation, vows of silence, they partake in heightened suffering to subjugate and separate from the body. As Evelyn Underhill described it eloquently in *Mysticism*,

> The death of selfhood in its narrow individualistic sense is, then, the primary object of mortification. All the twisted elements of character which foster the existence of this unreal yet complex creature are to be pruned away. Then, as with the trees of the forest, so with the spirit of man, strong new branches will spring into being, grow towards air and light.[30]

So mortification demonstrated will over body, and cleared the way for new ways of thinking and new ways of being. Just like pruning. Similarly, the road to mastery of any craft is the road of mastering the body, not in demonstrably extreme ways but in daily disciplines of mastery over time. The artist's path is made up of many small disciplines and deaths of self.

Modern psychology has helped us understand that each individual wears a mask, the mask given by family, by society, what Carl Jung called the *persona*. Over time we start to feel the dissonance between our outward mask and our inward self. Unfortunately, digital media, and especially social media, has exacerbated these divides between our outward and inner selves. Art can bring out this dissonance. This means there is something deeper within us which the current culture is not expressing, or even acknowledging exists. Our soul is resonating.

When creating art, the artist must get under the mask and open up the whole self. This is the powerful integration of the psyche that can happen with art - what is felt is what is being expressed, with no dissonance, all soul focused on and through the craft. With that expression can come a feeling of catharsis, like a weight was lifted, or a knot undone from the stomach. But first the ego must be overcome, because the ego is deathly afraid of such vulnerability.

And here we come to a common theme in mythology - as the hero goes deeper on the journey, more resistance is encountered from self and from society. As Maslow put it,

> What we have found during the last ten years or so is that, primarily, the sources of creativeness of the kind that we're really interested in, i.e., the generation of new ideas, are in the depths of human nature. We don't even have a vocabulary for it yet that's very good...
>
> This is a new frontier in the sense that most people don't know about it, and also in another very peculiar sense that has never occurred before in history. *This is something that not only we don't know about, but that we're afraid to know about.* That is, there is resistance to knowing about it.[18]

Fear. Maslow directly puts his finger on the source of much of the resistance. In *The Artist's Way*, Julia Cameron spends much of the book helping blocked artists work through their points of resistance, and she diagnoses it similarly,

> Fear is what blocks an artist. The fear of not being good enough. The fear of not finishing. The fear of failure and of success. The fear of beginning at all.[31]

Fear is the driver, but the resistance may be encountered many different ways. One way is by surrounding ourselves with what Cameron calls 'crazymakers', people that are always wrapped up in drama and try to take us with them. They make the water muddy and keep us from ever digging deep. There is a comfort in the drama so we sabotage ourselves by keeping them around. Ultimately, because we are artists, we always fear no longer being able to create. That the flow of creation will be turned off at the tap. But what is this fear, at its root? Death, fear of death, creative death. Otto Rank saw the fear of death as fundamental to creating, and denying death is embodied in humanity's concept of the soul.[8]

Fear also entwines with a strong sense of shame that arises as we open our soul without precondition. The feeling of what should be hidden being exposed. But there is also shame in being too selfish, overindulging our desires by focusing inward and creating art. There is a false humility that says we shouldn't reach high. There is an ever-present fear of failure, which is a huge obstacle to starting anything. If I start I might fail? And, as one approaches a goal, there is greater and greater fear of success. What would success actually mean for my life that I live, for my family?

This fear that rises up as an artist approaches their full potential is what Maslow called 'the Jonah complex'. In the Old Testament Jonah was called to be a prophet to Nineveh but he ran. The Jonah complex exists in each of us to some extent, because we know we have more potential within us than we've realized. Sometimes we glimpse the potential from the side of our vision, and it strikes terror into our heart. What if we reached it fully?

Jonah was swallowed down, down into the dark night for three days inside a whale, and then spat out onto the beach. Eventually Jonah did go to Nineveh, but it was a long journey, and by the time he got there his hair had turned certainly whiter, and he had become a different and wiser prophet. The Jonah complex is balanced by our drive for self-actualization, the drive to maximize our full potential that we occasionally glimpse. Maslow called it, "The desire to become more and more what one is, to become everything that one is capable of becoming."[32]

So there is a resistance but there is also a deep longing. Artists are driven by a dissatisfaction with a present shallow mode of being. The soul resonating to something deeper that must be expressed. These two forces of fear and longing pull at the artist. C.S. Lewis and Madeleine L'Engle were two modern writers who were students of, and adept at wielding, mythology. The closest thing to a biography C. S. Lewis left behind was *Surprised by Joy*, which he subtitled *The Shape of My Early Life*. Much of the book focuses on a deep feeling of longing that drove Lewis from a very young age to be on a spiritual journey. He encountered this longing in transcendental experiences of beauty with both art and nature. Because this feeling of longing was most clearly expressed in Norse mythology he began to call it "the Northernness". He describes one transcendental experience this way,

> Pure Northernness engulfed me: a vision of huge clear spaces hanging above the Atlantic in the endless twilight of Northern summer, remoteness, severity...

> And with that plunge back into my own past there arose at once, almost like heartbreak, the memory of Joy itself, the knowledge that I had once had what I had now lacked for years, that I was returning at last from exile and desert lands to my own country; and the distance of the Twilight of the Gods and the distance of my own past Joy, both unattainable, flowed together into a single unendurable sense of desire and loss.[33]

Madeleine L'Engle was very influenced by ancient Christian mystic traditions, and she encountered a similar fundamental longing,

> We are all strangers in a strange land, longing for home, but not quite knowing what or where home is. We glimpse it sometimes in our dreams, or as we turn a corner, and suddenly there is a strange, sweet familiarity that vanishes almost as soon as it comes.[34]

So there is a deep fundamental longing, desire, and heartbreak. As the artist approaches the soul these emotions surround it. There is a natural repulsion to entering into negative emotions which puts up another layer of resistance the artist must overcome. Loss is also present, as the soul feels any loss forever. The collective losses and regrets of one's life in the depths of the soul, accumulated and waiting. They wait for silence to come forward.

The way to the understanding of the soul is the way of contemplation. Most major religions throughout the world over time have had mystic branches of thought and practice that focus primarily on approaching the divine through experience and contemplation. These mystic traditions share a common approach. They teach disciples to walk a path of spiritual development and transcendence of present reality, often utilizing suffering and contemplation. Out of these mystic traditions have come some of the most transcendent music as well, from the ecstasies of the swirling sufi to the somber chanting of the monks. I believe these mystic traditions hold many secrets of transcendence that would serve our modern societies well to understand.

In her comparative study of Christian mythology in *Mysticism*, Evelyn Underhill identifies five characteristic stages of mystic spiritual development:

> (1) *The awakening*
> The awakening of the self to consciousness of divine reality. This experience, usually abrupt and well-marked, is accompanied by intense feelings of joy and exaltation.

(2) *Purgation*

The self, aware for the first time of divine beauty, realizes by contrast its own finiteness and imperfection, the manifold illusions in which it is immersed, the immense distance which separates it from the One. Its attempts to eliminate by discipline and mortification all that stands in the way of its progress towards union with God constitute *Purgation:* a state of pain and effort.

(3) *Illumination*

When by purgation the self has become detached from the "things of sense" ...it has awakened to knowledge of teality, has struggled up the harsh and difficult path to the mouth of the cave. Now it looks upon the sun. This is *Illumination:* a state which includes in itself many of the stages of contemplation, "degrees of orison," visions and adventures of the soul described by St. Teresa and other mystical writers.

(4) *The Dark Night of the Soul.*

In the development of the great and strenuous seekers after God, this is followed—or sometimes intermittently accompanied—by the most terrible of all the experiences of the mystic way: the final and complete purification of the self, which is called by some contemplatives the "mystic pain" or "mystic death," by others the purification of the spirit or *Dark Night of the Soul*.

(5) *Union*

The true goal of the mystic quest. In this state the absolute life is not merely perceived and enjoyed by the self, as in Illumination: but is *one* with it. This is the end towards which all the previous oscillations of consciousness have tended. It is a state of equilibrium, of purely spiritual life; characterized by peaceful joy, by enhanced powers, by intense certitude.[30]

Note that these stages of development closely resemble the stages of Joseph Campbell's hero's journey. And that is why mythology becomes quite useful, because each individual's journey into their own soul is heroic, and filled with danger. But underlying all of that is a call to go deeper, a yearning, a longing, and glimpses of transcendent truth, so ultimately the artist must embark. Along the way there is suffering, contemplation, and transcendence; then down into the dark night and the soul dies a death; then out into greater transcendence.

The mystic journey can occur at multiple levels, over many different time spans, repeated as the mystic moves deeper through the layers of the soul and is transformed by the process. Edwin Starbuck compiled a comparative study of religious experiences into *Psychology of Religion*, and he described the common conversion experiences this way:

> Conversion is primarily an *unselfing*. The first birth of the individual is into his own little world. He is controlled by the deep-seated instincts of self-preservation and self-enlargement—instincts which are, doubtless, a direct inheritance from his brute ancestry. The universe is organized around his own personality as a centre.
>
> Conversion is the larger world-consciousness now pressing in on the individual consciousness. Often it breaks in suddenly and becomes a great new revelation. This is the first aspect of conversion: the person emerges from a smaller limited world of existence into a larger world of being. His life becomes swallowed up in a larger whole.[35]

This realization that leads to transformation can be sudden and quite painfully stark. For example, an epiphany that a whole life has been wasted up to the present time. Although painful, this kind of breakthrough is a vital encounter with truth, what Flannery O'Connor called moments of 'dark grace.' In her writings O'Connor often used these epiphanies of the ugliness of one's own behavior to shake her characters out of the present stupor. You are forced to look at what you have become. Or what you have done. Or what you have lost.

As Julia Cameron put it,

> ..the old you is leaving and grieving, while the new you celebrates and grows strong. As with any rupture there is both tension and relief. Long-seated depression breaks up like an ice flow. Long-frozen feelings thaw, melt, cascade, flood, and often overrun their container (you). You may find yourself feeling volatile and changeable. You are.
>
> Be prepared for bursts of tears and of laughter. A certain giddiness may accompany sudden stabs of loss. Think of yourself as an accident victim walking away from the crash: your old life has crashed and burned; your new life isn't apparent yet. You may feel yourself to be temporarily without a vehicle. Just keep walking.[31]

The lens of the Christian mystic saw suffering and death and then rebirth as a natural part of their journey towards spiritual transcendence, indeed a necessary part, so they would ritualize the dark night of the soul and thus bear this burden communally. Although the community can help bear the weight of darkness, this journey is an inward one that is fundamentally spiritual. Each journey is unique. There is no way to know how deep the valley will be, or how long it will last, one must only go through.

The ego dissolves into union, this is the ultimate goal of the mystic. But for the artist, the highest goal is the purposeful channeling of the unconscious into creative power through the ego. Like damming up a meandering river, power can be focused and captured. Negative emotions of the unconscious, like fear, panic, domination, anger, can be utilized without letting them take control. Artists over time have utilized the toolbox of the mystics to achieve greater self-knowledge and control.

The mystic's most fundamental tool to reach this state of control is contemplation. From Underhill's *Mysticism*,

> Contemplation is the mystic's medium. It is an extreme form of withdrawal of attention from the external world and total dedication of the mind which also, in various degrees and ways, conditions the creative activity of musician, painter, and poet; releasing the faculty by which he can apprehend the Good and Beautiful, enter into communion with the Real.
>
> We cannot long read the works of the mystics without coming across descriptions - often first-hand descriptions of great psychological interest - of the processes through which the self must pass, the discipline which it must undertake in the course of acquiring the art of contemplation.
>
> Most of these descriptions differ in detail; in the divisions adopted, the emotions experienced, the number of "degrees" through which the subject passes, from the first painful attempt to gather up its faculties to the supreme point at which it feels itself to be "lost in God".[30]

There, in the quiet, we must wrestle with our own self and our own wounds. We must understand who we have been, and where we are headed. In silence, contemplation teaches us to connect to our emotions, our soul, and ultimately what lies beneath in our unconscious. Contemplation proceeds great art, because we must first descend into the unexpressed truth before it can be embodied in a particular craft.

John of the Cross, a Renaissance-era Spanish monk, wrote multiple books about the mystical journey, including the influential *Dark Night of the Soul* and *Ascent of Mount Carmel*. He also wrote two books of poetry, including this beautiful opening from the poem The Dark Night,

> Upon an obscure night
> Fevered with Love's anxiety
> (O hapless, happy plight!)
> I went, none seeing me,
> Forth from my house, where all things quiet be.[36]

THE MYTHOLOGY OF THE ARTIST

Each of us must walk this journey through our unconscious ourselves. Over time we will find the fog begins to clear, and the connection to the emotions becomes more vivid. We become unafraid to commune with ourself. And in that communion the mind is quieted, resistance decreases, and our unconscious opens outward and begins to 'flow'.

The artist can descend into the state of flow with creativity out of the unconscious. Flow is basically the connection of the unconscious creativity directly to the artistic craft.

Hungarian psychologist Mihaly Csíkszentmihályi is the modern author of the concept of creative flow. In studies across highly creative people he defined six characteristics of the state of flow:

1. Intense and focused concentration on the present moment
2. Merging of action and awareness
3. A loss of reflective self-consciousness
4. A sense of personal control or agency over the situation or activity
5. A distortion of temporal experience, one's subjective experience of time is altered
6. Experience of the activity as intrinsically rewarding[37]

The state of flow feels like being completely and totally in the moment, doing what one does best with all of your being. It's fully being present, so much in the present that nothing else exists. It's feeling all five senses with full clarity. Creating within the flow brings a naturally joyful feeling. It's a feeling of tremendous power being used for good, which is like a feeling of joy. With power to create anything, to destroy and re-align anything, the artist wields craft with mastery connected to the soul to create something of significance and beauty.

Creative ideas emerge out of a relaxed state of mind. Research led by Katahira and Yamazaki in Japan found that people in the state of flow (solving a problem) had increased alpha and theta brain waves.[38] Alpha brain waves are connected to daydreaming, and theta brainwaves to the first stage of sleep. Think back to the last time you daydreamed. That was a relaxed feeling, no danger, or anger or threat. It felt hazy, like the self letting go a little bit. Everything in the body is relaxed, and the mind wanders. Wandering the path, this is the beginning of the realm of creative ideas.

Sometimes an idea will incubate for a long time before it emerges, and when it finally does it could be when we're taking a shower or doing yoga. This is when dopamine is releasing, and the rational left brain gets somewhat distracted, our unconscious can take over and start to flow. Archimedes was soaking in a warm bath when he shouted, "eureka!", and that story has mythologized the creative idea for eighteen hundred years. The reason that mythology has persisted is because it is true, and continues to be true. Jonah Lehrer, neuroscientist and author of *Imagine: How Creativity Works*, explains it this way,

> What explains the creative benefits of relaxation and booze? The answer involves the surprising advantage of not paying attention. Although we live in an age that worships focus - we are always forcing ourselves to concentrate, chugging caffeine - this approach can inhibit the imagination. We might be focused, but we're probably focused on the wrong answer.
>
> And this is why relaxation helps: It isn't until we're soothed in the shower or distracted by the stand-up comic that we're able to turn the spotlight of attention inward, eavesdropping on all those random associations unfolding in the far reaches of the brain's right hemisphere. When we need an insight, those associations are often the source of the answer.[39]

In relaxation an idea rises, the germ of an idea, and then it is worked over, shaped, and molded. The idea is merged with other disconnected strands of thought. The artist's mind is engaged and relaxed with complete flexibility. The artist needs a supple mind that can zoom in and zoom out, take differing lenses as needed. Supple enough to be able to play with various points of view. Out of the playfulness new ideas emerge, are thrown together, are torn apart, and then put together in new ways.

When an idea first emerges it is extremely moldable, but also tenuous. That moment of emergence is a very special and fleeting moment. It will bubble up but then can be ephemeral, and quickly fade. Unless you reach out consciously and grab onto it, hold onto it, focus on it, it can fade into the black of a thousand other emerging ideas. Or a distracted moment could let it slip away. What seems like a better idea could emerge, but that turns out to be a mirage and the original idea is gone.

In that moment of flow there's almost an inebriated feeling. In *Twilight of the Idols*, Nietzsche said that for art to exist, "a certain physiological precondition is indispensable: intoxication."[40] In the moment of flow, we tell ourself, "don't worry, I'll remember that." It's a lie, you won't. Is this a way we self-sabotage? You won't remember that exact feeling, of that moment in time, when it emerged. It has special magic, because it is truly an impression of the soul at a particular moment in time, and so it must be treated reverently. Experienced songwriters will carry a tape recorder, so if an idea emerges when they are driving, or running, it can be captured to be worked over later. It takes 30 seconds to capture an idea, just capture it and then finish your run. You won't remember it later.

Back before the age of tape recorders, Shah Abdul Latif Bhittai was a sufi artist, musician, and poet in Pakistan. He wrote one song that was so beautiful, his followers decided it could never be forgotten, and must be preserved exactly as it was written. So they played the song every single day, in the same place where it was originally composed, from 1752 until the present day, as William Dalrymple shows in his documentary *Sufi Soul: The Mystic Music of Islam*.[41] Watching the video it becomes immediately apparent why the Shah's disciples acted as they did. It was the only rational reaction to a moment of tremendous magic and power. I can imagine them saying with excitement, "Everyone learn this song, watch the Shah closely, we will play this now every single day. Forever."

When a unique idea emerges, take hold of it gently and turn it around in your head. At first emergence ideas are very fluid, so play with it for a while. Let it simmer. Focus on it loosely, think around it and over it, play. Don't bring out your inner censor yet, keep that away for a while. Let it emerge without judgement, because it's not done yet, it's only beginning. Write it down, record it, draw it, build it, put it into a different format as you play. Keep it like a secret for a while, until it feels right, and then discuss it with others, as writer/scientist Isaac Asimov said,

> My feeling is that as far as creativity is concerned, isolation is required. The creative person is, in any case, continually working at it. His mind is shuffling his information at all times, even when he is not conscious of it. (The famous example of Kekule working out the structure of benzene in his sleep is well-known.)
>
> The presence of others can only inhibit this process, since creation is embarrassing. For every new good idea you have, there are a hundred, ten thousand foolish ones, which you naturally do not care to display.
>
> Nevertheless, a meeting of such people may be desirable for reasons other than the act of creation itself.[42]

So, following Asimov, nurture it, share it with a few, and think on it. Take care it doesn't solidify - sometimes if you let an idea sit in one shape too long then your brain becomes stuck. If it still needs work then play with it, merge it, shape it, and then document it once you have reached a stopping point. But don't lose the emotion - this is the only important part, the initial emotion is the key cornerstone that you will build upon, so document the emotion. Once you have preserved the emotion you can stop at any time and come back to it, so if energy runs out then take a break. Later, when you are back in your logical left brain, you can take your censor out again and get a completely new detached point of view. This way you use both left and right brain cognitive powers on the same idea and in their respective strengths. Record the initial emotion, and then ruminate on that emotion and complexify it.

Out of the unconscious flows creative ideas with pure originality. The flow is constant, some of the ideas will be useful and some will not, but more is always behind. Mastery of this flow of creativity can occur on multiple levels of complexity, and it takes time to master utilizing creativity at multiple levels. Once you learn to control flow you can learn how to change lenses with which to aim, achieving deep levels of complexity.

Consider a violinist who plays Mahler's Symphony No. 4 with tremendous expressiveness. That is one level of creative complexity. But consider now, Mahler, who created that symphony from scratch and imagined it with that original vitality. That is the second level. But now consider Haydn, who created the original concept of the symphony, in which form Mahler is writing. That is the third level, which is the creation of a new branch of craft. From Picasso's influence on painting, to Bob Dylan's influence on pop music. The existing craft is no longer sufficient, so to be completely original the soul of the artist just creates a new branch of craft out of itself and for itself. The highest level of creativity, or to put it another way, creativity at every level of complexity.

The way to reach this level of creativity is to independently become a master of working in all three levels, and then work over the problem one level at a time. The only way to learn to work on a new level is to do it: attempt something bigger than you have done before. Many times over. Eventually you will learn to control these attempts. Controlling creativity at multiple levels is like aiming through a telephoto lens that you can zoom in and out. To look at them again:

Level 1, the lowest level of originality, would be painting a beautiful watercolor landscape. It has beauty, and originality at the granular level, like in the way the colors interplay. But a watercolor landscape has also been done many times before, and so originality is naturally low. This level of creativity is also low risk, because you took no real risk to create in a style that has been done many times before.

Level 2 is an intermediate level of originality, and this would be like Van Gogh introducing a radical new type of impressionism. It's transcendent and tremendously impactful. But we still place him as an impressionist painter, more or less perfecting techniques of brushstroke and texture that many other artists were also working in. This level has a moderately high risk of failure, because you are pushing into something new, as Van Gogh saw in his time (with resistance from the French establishment).

Level 3, the highest level of originality, is like Picasso, who invented multiple styles, each of which went on to become their own genre. Or Einstein, who originated so many ideas we are still working to confirm if all of them are true. This level is pure originality, pioneering where no one has ventured even once before, into the black darkness with only a candle. This level has the highest potential of risk, failure, but also glory. For this level there is no in-between. The person is either brilliant or mad, because it requires such dedication there is nothing else left behind.

Confounding this system is the fact that emotions are different than original ideas, but when they have clarity they can be astoundingly original. As the soul emerges originality increases. This means that performers who dig deep into emotion don't necessarily have to write originally to be original. So an actor in a play may not have written the play, but by becoming lost in the character and drawing on their own experiences and feelings they can achieve a very high level of emotional originality. Itzhak Perlman is an Israeli violinist who contracted polio as a child and was left confined to a chair. He latched onto the violin and immediately merged with it, giving his first concert at age 10 and appearing on the Ed Sullivan show at age 13. Watching him perform is to see the highest level of emotional involvement, as he plays from the whole body with complete expression of his soul. He may not have written the sonata, but he is a completely unique embodiment of it.

All three levels need to be addressed to achieve Level 3, so Level 3 could be envisioned as the top of a pyramid. Master artists always try to open up their mind to create on Level 3, because the higher you aim the higher your ceiling could potentially be. You aim for Level 3 and open your mind to try to create a whole new genre of music, then you move down into Level 2 and create the most beautiful song that could exist in that completely new genre of music, and finally move to Level 1 where you perfect the lyrics and arrangement with beauty. Sometimes you will need to take a break - a shower, a walk, maybe even days or months before you can reset your mind to clearly move into the next level. Each level is basically a shift of lens, so a lens reset is needed between levels.

This is why some master artists of the Renaissance had 'assembly lines', basically understudies who did all of the Level 1 work and assisted with Level 2 creation. The master spent most of the time on Level 2/3, the world of original ideas. However, if you look at some bands you can see a perfect blending of personalities working at different levels. Rush is an iconic intellectual's rock band. Lead singer Geddy Lee is the one who originates the sweeping melodic emotions, and then drummer Neil Peart builds complex song-poems out of them.

One example of this process of creative partners provoking a lens change is when Paul McCartney wrote the beautiful acoustic ballad, "Yesterday". The core idea just emerged, he woke up with the melody and chords in his head, as if out of a dream. He said, "I didn't believe I'd written it. I thought maybe I'd heard it before, it was some other tune, and I went around for weeks playing the chords of the song for people."[43] But he had written it. It resonated so deeply in his unconscious that it felt like deja vu and originality at the same time. He made it into a little love song at first, "Scrambled eggs / oh my baby how I love your legs…". Silly, classic Paul, in a relaxed playful mood, singing a sentimental song about breakfast and sex. But he was able to capture the special feeling, and then bring back up the emotion and work on it over time. As John later said,

> The song was around for months and months before we finally completed it. Every time we got together to write songs for a recording session, this one would come up. We almost had it finished. Paul wrote nearly all of it, but we just couldn't find the right title. We called it "Scrambled Eggs" and it became a joke between us. We made up

> our minds that only a one-word title would suit, we just couldn't find the right one. Then one morning Paul woke up and the song and the title were both there, completed. I was sorry in a way, we'd had so many laughs about it.[44]

The original idea was beautiful and iconic, potentially a Level 2/3 kind of emotion. But it didn't become complete until Paul changed lenses, to the detail of Level 1, and drilled into the lyrics, turning it into the beautiful moving piece of art that it became. John often drove Paul to push out into the next level of creativity, and vice versa. As a side note, there is another level at work on those Beatles records, we could call it Level 0.5 - the phenomenal audio engineering work of George Martin, the 'sixth Beatle'.

Most things director Stanley Kubrick did were at Level 2 or 3. No one had done a movie like *Space Odyssey 2001*. It took five years to create and was entirely unique, from its tone to its pacing to the astounding cinematography. Creative at every level. But then *Barry Lyndon* was shot all by candlelight with NASA-designed wide-aperture lenses, a period piece that was completely different in tone, pace, and feel, each shot like a living Renaissance painting. Kubrick did not discriminate, he was simply pushing for originality, emotion, and straining against what was conventional. He had dialed into his own creative process and became a master of changing lenses, carefully crafting within the flow until he perfected the art at one level, and then changing lenses again.

At the highest level of originality there is no map, the waters are all uncharted. No one has been this way before, so there is nothing to build on. Casting out into the darkness, creating something purely original is a slow but tremendously rewarding process of trying many many things. As we playfully experiment many ideas emerge, we eliminate bad ideas, and slowly over time we end up with good ideas, and then eventually quite excellent and polished ideas. As David Jones said in *The Aha! Moment: A Scientist's Take on Creativity*,

> Most ideas fail in practice, so everyone trying to be creative has to live with lots of failures. It doesn't matter; you discard the ones that don't work.
>
> Precisely the same style of thinking applies in science and technology. You cannot, in logic, deduce a theory from the data it must explain or a machine from the need it must fill. So a scientist or technologist dreams up possible theories or possible machines and sees whether they fit. Most of the time they don't. Sometimes you have to devise an experiment, or even a whole program of them, to clarify the problem. I have wasted vast amounts of time asking the wrong question or building an apparatus that merely shuts off one stupid area of inquiry. But even with hindsight I cannot advise any other way to go.[45]

Moving upward through the levels is often simply the natural transformation of the skill of the artist over time. Most artists will start below Level 1, they will imitate something well-known, for example they will trace a drawing with no originality and no risk. Then small steps of creativity. Amateurs, first starting out, will accept the first original idea that emerges. Later, with experience, they will start to understand how to create art more true to self. The way they do this is by listening to their own emotions as they create. Creating while listening. By the time an artist has been creating for twenty years they will have often found their own unique voice, completely original, no one else could have made it. By that time they are potentially in the second Level. If one of them forges a new genre and category of art, then Level 3 is a possibility.

However, the gulf between Level 2 and Level 3 is very wide. Opening up a new branch of craft is a tremendous accomplishment that only a relatively few artists will do every century, although we all aspire to Level 3 and hopefully will improve at achieving it in our lifetime. It is an overarching goal, not a burden, just an ideal. Master works of art elicit awe in us, because we can see the height of human potential. Artists operating at optimum capacity, with maximum creativity, plus experience over time, can create Level 3 works of art. However, occasionally an artist can go to Level 3 with less experience if they are uniquely talented, emotional, and uninhibited, a shooting star like Janis Joplin and Jeff Buckley.

The gulf is wide, but the effort can sometimes seem small. Mastering creativity can at times feel like learning to play golf, where the harder an amateur swings the less likely they are to swing well. Creativity requires that kind of relaxed focus, the mind fully engaged, and that takes practice and time to learn to do consistently. But over time, relaxing into the flow, letting your thoughts roll over you, you can connect to your emotions and begin to feel those ideas that stir the soul. The master creates a groove that has become so smooth it is easy to ride in, easy to move. Creativity improves with practice. The feeling of creating becomes easier to slip in and out of. The resistance decreases, or at least we learn tricks to overcome it.

Ultimately, we can then ask, what is great art, or how can we know it when we produce it? Moral philosopher and author of *War and Peace*, Leo Tolstoy, argues that only what is supremely impactful emotionally can be even called art. It must change your state of mind, and all else is "counterfeit". He tackled the question in the small but deep *What Is Art?*,

> Art in our society has become perverted to such a degree that not only has bad art come to be considered good, but even the very notion of what art is has been lost, so that, in order to speak of art in our society, one must first of all distinguish true art from counterfeit.
>
> One indisputable sign that distinguishes true art from counterfeit is the infectiousness of art. If a man, without any effort on his own part and without any change in his situation, having read, heard, or seen a work by another man, experiences a state of mind which unites him to this man and with others who perceive the object of art in the same way as he does, then the object which calls up such a state is an object of art.[46]

We can apply this lens of creative mastery to works of art in any field of study. However, there isn't much use in trying to determine which past works of art are most creatively transcendent. We should have grace for humans of the past and remember each artwork was of full power in its own time, through that lens. The purpose of discussing this rubric is only to show the ideal, that it is possible to truly master creativity in itself, as its own thing, in our time. It is possible to become a master at creativity, and some before us have done it. It can be done. Once we are at the level of creative mastery we should aim very high, we should be creating new branches of art nonstop. The creative explosion of the 60s, which truly was an explosion in music from jazz to folk to britpop, is possible anytime - we are human as they were human, each with a soul.

Mastery of craft is a long road, every great teacher is honest about that. It takes time to master anything. Usually the first few years are spent getting the basic movements. The history of the craft must be learned, and all aspects must be understood. Then there is a second level creative process, where multiple original ideas are put together into an affecting narrative, and risk-taking increases with confidence. And sometimes, an artist can break into the third level, and make something completely new. No genre, no category, something that has never existed. A new branch emerges. At the highest level of the craft the artist often begins looking at all disciplines, as some are thousands of years more developed than others, and the creative mind can use all of it.

Up until the modern period the path of the young artist was through apprenticeship in the workshops of masters. They would begin an apprenticeship around ten years of age. These apprentices disciplined themselves to various technical aspects of the craft, like grinding pigments for the master's paint, for as long as eight years. But they also were immersed in the way the master artist created from the depths of the soul with originality and intent. So the master embodied knowledge of self for the student, and thus a way of interacting with the soul was passed on over time.

In his book *Mastery,* Robert Greene looked at the road to mastery by well-known artists and scientists throughout time, from Mozart to Darwin. He found a similar story: to begin on the path you must first find your calling, meaning something you innately love. Then moving into that calling the artist submits to apprenticeship, and eventually tries to absorb some of the master's power. After that the student goes out into a broader worldly path of self-discovery and challenge. The final step is Mastery, which is where you, "fuse the intuitive with the rational." And that is the ultimate goal of mastery, to fuse the intuitive with craft.

And then, after much hard practice, traveling through many deep valleys and over steep mountains, the artist will sometimes stumble into a beautiful meadow, suddenly on wings of the wind. As Greene eloquently puts it,

> Throughout history we read of Masters in every conceivable form of human endeavor describing a sensation of suddenly possessing heightened intellectual powers after years of immersion in their field.
>
> Through intense absorption in a particular field over a long period of time, Masters come to understand all of the parts involved in what they are studying. They reach a point where all of this has become internalized and they are no longer seeing the parts, but gain an intuitive feel for the whole. They literally see or sense the dynamic.[47]

So the craft becomes a kind of meditation, a mindfulness in the moment of the craft as the artist begins to simply embody it. Working in the present, intuitively, eyes metaphorically closed, in the body and through the craft. If we can get into this mindset then self-discipline becomes meditative joy, embodying the craft and working to mastery becomes innately meaningful. And then as we express our craft to others we find greater meaning again, in the pouring out.

SUFFERING AND TRANSCENDENCE

American professor of literature Joseph Campbell studied myths and looked for common elements between them, to better understand our human tendencies that created them. He compiled them into the book *The Hero with a Thousand Faces,* published in 1949.[48] His comparative mythology found most cultures had a variant of what he called the 'hero's journey', summarized in this helpful diagram from Wikimedia Commons. It shows the hero descending from the *known* into the *unknown*, with the help of guardians and mentors:

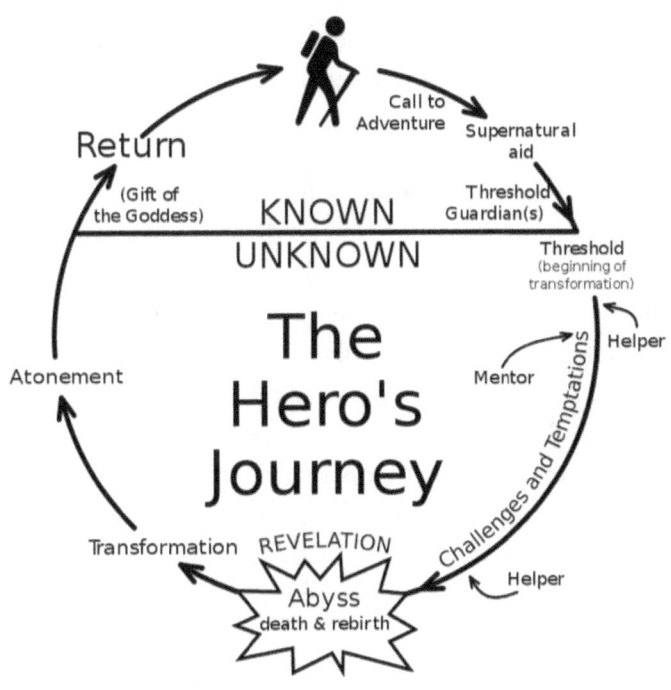

It starts with a call to adventure that resonates with something deep in the soul of the hero, who then sets out on the journey. Early on a mentor and/or a guardian will equip them and help them go deeper. The artist will then endure many trials and challenges, victories and defeats, dragons and monsters, culminating in a death of self and death of the initial call in the depths of the abyss. Out of this state of struggle can come a rebirth of soul as something brand new emerges. Atonement and restoration follows, and a new phase begins. The artist has undergone the hero's journey, only one time of many, and is reborn. Each great artist will likely undergo some variant of this journey many times over.

Why does this mythological pattern exist in most every culture? Because humans are biological organisms who change over time, encounter obstacles, suffering, and defeats, and ultimately long to achieve certain higher, greater things during their lifetimes. Our story shows our journey, as we are each travelers through time. What we long for will shift and change as we interact with the world over time, and the world will also change. Mythology has a power to help us work through and understand our difficult journeys, struggles, transformations, deaths, and rebirths, over time. These stories were told around fires to calm the troubled and confused souls. Mythology can place our life into context and reveal deeper hidden truths.

The hero's journey is true because each of us must descend into our self, into the unknown, as illustrated in the diagram. Knowledge of the self necessarily means beginning to become aware of your own inner shadow side as it unfolds over time. One thing readily apparent in studying various cultural mythologies, as well as the 'lived' mythology of artists' lives, is that humans are fundamentally flawed and self-destructive. We can destroy the things we love, and we can also destroy ourselves from the inside out. Great art is created out of traversing that pain and suffering, while encountering and wrestling with the self. The self as both creator and destroyer. Like Jacob wrestling with the angel that ultimately leaves his hip deformed. All of this creation and destruction lies beneath the seemingly calm surface of the body.

Francis Bacon was a socialite Irish painter in London, very calm and charming on the surface but he painted violent, obliterated, screaming faces. His paintings are so visceral they can cause you to gasp or flinch on first sight. He was trying to reconcile his outward and inward selves through his work, all the time. As he tried to put it in words in an interview from 1972,

> I think that life is violent and most people turn away from that side of it in an attempt to live a life that is screened. But I think they are merely fooling themselves. I mean, the act of birth is a violent thing, and the act of death is a violent thing. And, as you surely have observed, the very act of living is violent. For example, there is self-violence in the fact that I drink much too much. But I feel ever so strongly that an artist must learn to be nourished by his passions and by his despairs. These things alter an artist whether for the good or for the better or the worse. It must alter him. The feelings of desperation and unhappiness are more useful to an artist than the feeling of contentment, because desperation and unhappiness stretch your whole sensibility.[49]

Many artists will, at one time or another, be plunged deeply into terrible despair and darkness like Francis Bacon. A crumbling of dreams and death of vision, when the self is forced to let go. Sometimes, out of this valley of the shadow of death will come the most truly transcendent art. Beethoven made many beautiful symphonies, but only created the transcendent *Ninth* after losing his whole artistic sensory world by going deaf. The suicide of Picasso's close friend brought on the mournfully transcendent 'blue period' paintings. Suffering can sometimes open up the soul in new ways. When that occurs, if the artist has been devoted to the craft with discipline, then a new depth of expression can begin to emerge in a new mode of creation. It is never too late in life to begin to emerge.

Mythologies often contain stories of metamorphosis, a transformation that must be undergone to enter a new phase of one's life. Just as spiritual mystics of the past sought change by inflicting suffering, so we see, on the other side of tremendous suffering, the artist can emerge transformed. Sometimes this is a cataclysmic event that changes the course of the artists' life.

Frida Kahlo was a talented sketch artist at the age of 18 when the wooden bus she was riding collided with a streetcar, sending a piece of an iron handrail through her pelvis. She survived, but was confined to two years of forced bedrest, forced to give up her dream of becoming a doctor. During that time in bed she began to create small paintings of tremendous surreal power, dreamlike representations of suffering and pain.

In her self-portrait *The Broken Column* we see the artist naked in a desert wasteland. As if by x-ray we see through to her spine fractured in multiple places. Straps wrap around her like a girdle as if to keep her from falling apart, and random nails pierce her skin. A horizontal veil of tears comes down out of both eyes.

An artist intimately familiar with suffering was southern American writer Flannery O'Connor, who was diagnosed with lupus, which had killed her father, at age 27. Her most insightful and devastating short stories were written while battling that illness over many years on her mother's dairy farm. As she put it in a letter to a friend in 1956,

> I've never been anywhere but sick. In a sense sickness is a place, more instructive than a long trip to Europe, and it's always a place where there's no company, where nobody can follow. Sickness before death is a very appropriate thing and I think those who don't have it miss one of God's mercies.[50]

From Vincent Van Gogh to Kurt Cobain, Sylvia Plath to Edgar Allan Poe, Elliot Smith to Nick Drake, many of the most uniquely creative artists seem to have been in a state of constant wrestling with their own bodies and their own minds. Too sensitive to walk in this world without suffering. To study the lives of artists is to see sickness, addiction, depression, grief, and loss. This suffering eventually can break down the shell around the self, the ego, and the soul can seep through in glimpses of transcendence. Edvard Munch, who created one of the most quintessential paintings of modern existential angst in *The Scream*, saw the suffering as necessarily entwined with his art,

> My fear of life is necessary to me, as is my illness. Without anxiety and illness, I am a ship without a rudder....My sufferings are part of my self and my art. They are indistinguishable from me, and their destruction would destroy my art.[51]

Suffering seems to be entwined with art for as long as art history goes back. Lines begin to blur between mental illness and creativity, as so many creative people, from Beethoven to Plath to David Foster Wallace, were known for their mental illness. In a recent meta-analysis of 36 studies in *Perspectives on Psychological Science*, Christa Taylor found that creative people were statistically more likely to have a diagnosis of a mood disorder, especially depression and bi-polar disorder.[52] However, having a mood disorder did not increase the likelihood of being creative, so it is hard to know which is actually the causal agent. But those of us who are artists, we see the correlation. As a recent study on mood disorders in the life of German poet Goethe summarized it thusly,

> In Goethe's life poetic incubation, illumination and elaboration seemed to be associated with psychic labilisation and dysthymia, sometimes with depressive episodes in a clinical sense. Thus, creative work was on the one hand triggered by depressive and dysthymic moods and served on the other hand to cope with depressive moods as well as with suicidal tendencies.[53]

Daniel Johnston was a classic example of intertwined creativity and mental illness, producing tape after tape of brilliant contemplative pop from his parent's basement in Texas in the 1980s. Most of his best recordings were made to cassette tape on a $59 Sanyo monaural boombox, plaintively singing with piano and a cheap chord organ. These albums were recorded in between stays in psychiatric institutions with schizophrenia and bipolar disorder. The documentary *The Devil and Daniel Johnston* is an insightful exposition of Daniel's deep and open soul. He wrote brutally honest lyrics, this from *Despair Came Knocking* in 1983,

> Despair came knocking at my door
> And I let her in for a while
> She sat on the couch and began smoking
> She said nothing
> Suddenly I felt tired
> I began to feel tired
> And all of the sudden
> The room seemed dingy and dirty
> Despair came knocking
> And I let her in for awhile[54]

Entwined like the serpents on the staff, mental illness sometimes comes along with creativity, and we don't fully understand how they interact. But the uniqueness of the artist is wrapped within the disorders, and pain, and flaws, and regrets. Daniel Johnston wrote beautifully about despair because he knew despair very well. He knew despair from his battle with mental illness in his parent's basement. And on a $59 tape recorder he created something transcendent, still affecting people today. From his dark night of the soul, we can hear his voice, it sounds childlike and openhearted, but also hurt and broken. As artists, all we can do is open our soul, speak truth, and try to bring light.

Many highly creative people are also highly sensitive to their environment and to stimuli around them. High sensitivity is like a superpower that comes with great weakness. It can be used for good, but often it results in torment. Torment from the body, and torment from a harsh world. No matter what the time and place, the highly sensitive person will be highly sensitive to the flow of things around them. So it's nearly impossible to separate out the torment and suffering of these artists from who they are, it is in their essence of soul. At times it can become a superpower - immediately in touch with your emotions when experimenting with orchestration for a new song, sensitive to how the intertwining instruments will fit the mood of the moment. Other times the sound of the bus brakes, metal on metal squealing, will ruin a whole afternoon.

Alice Flaherty was a neurologist who worked with Parkinson patients. In 1998 she lost twin sons to a miscarriage, and then proceeded to fall down a rabbit hole of perception,

> My postpartum mood disorder, which had several manic as well as the more typical depressed features, came after I had given birth prematurely to twin boys who had died. They were so small - one grasped my finger before he died, and his hand hardly fit around it. For ten days I was filled with sorrow. Then, suddenly, as if someone had thrown a switch, I was wildly agitated, full of ideas, all of them pressing to be written down. The world was flooded with meaning. I believed I had unique access to the secrets of the Kingdom of Sorrow, about which I had an obligation to enlighten my - very tolerant - friends and colleagues through essays and letters.[55]

For the next four months she, "ricocheted between euphoria and terror." During bouts of mania, she was gripped with hypergraphia, which is an overwhelming need to write one's thoughts down. And she wrote a lot, thousands of pages, which eventually became *The Midnight Disease: The Drive to Write, Writer's Block, and the Creative Brain*. These symptoms interacted with the medications that were tried on her. She describes it vividly,

> On good days, ideas would wake me at four in the morning, tendrils of words coiling around me like some heady perfume. It was as if a door had opened onto a hot wind from the tropics, the sort of wind that propels ships carrying peacock feathers and rubies and apes and incense. On bad days, the words were like a charnel house through which I had to search for the bodies of missing people. In either case, the desire to write was overpowering.[55]

Dr. Flaherty eventually went on to do research into dopamine release into the brain, and its effect on creative urges. She found that hypergraphia is also affiliated with temporal lobe epilepsy, which causes Geschwind Syndrome, a cluster of five personality traits: hypergraphia; a deepened emotional life (hyper-philosophical or hyper-religious); emotional volatility; altered sexuality; and over-inclusiveness or extreme talkativeness. Some scholars have postulated that Nietzsche suffered from this group of symptoms.[56] But even though Dr. Flaherty could describe and understand her experiences in biological terms, she still considered it transcendent and life-altering. She went through a dark night of the soul and emerged with greater knowledge, and now she has dedicated her life to studying what it was. A scientist pursuing the transcendent.

Similarly, the connection between creativity and migraine appears strong. Artists who have suffered from migraines include Debussy, Wagner, Van Gogh, Monet, Virginia Woolf, and Emily Dickenson. The feeling of a migraine is like the worst pain you've had, with pressure, in the head, for hours. You become extremely sensitive to light and sound. Migraine pain sometimes gets to a point where the sufferer is certain it's beyond bearable, and then the pain will still continue to increase. As writer Joan Didion said, "That no one dies of migraine seems, to someone deep into an attack, an ambiguous blessing."[57] Along with migraine often comes an aura, which can bring manic like feelings before the onset of the migraine.

The aura is like the sword of Damocles, the harbinger of doom, a rush of mania before descent into sheer darkness and pain for hours. The aura has its own special awfulness of knowing the pain that lies unavoidable ahead. Helpless, waiting, the aura leaves you contemplating doom. Auras can also be visual and hallucinogenic, light that ripples in colorful ways. 'Alice In Wonderland Syndrome' is the feeling of distortion in perceptions that can come with a migraine, and Louis Carroll was another famous migraine sufferer.[58] As author Lydia Ruffles described it,

> It's really difficult for me to divorce my migraine from my creativity. I think it still has a big influence on the way I use language. I often say I feel like each migraine collapses

and rebuilds your reality and perception. It can make your brain feel things that you didn't think it could feel and your mind gets sort of stretchy.[59]

In the aura phase, the sufferer becomes extremely sensitive. Synesthesia can take over, the crossing over of the senses where sounds can be seen and smells can be felt. Synesthesia is also connected to disturbances in the temporal lobe, and some level of synesthesia is a normal everyday occurrence for certain people. The list of artists who experience synesthesia is long, and musicians are specially affected, from Liszt and Bernstein to Duke Ellington and Billy Joel. Itzhak Perlman described the crossing of sensations and the usefulness of it in a 2012 interview with Psychology Today,

> I know that I can describe certain sounds with color. It's not music - it's notes, it's single sounds. So if I hear a particular sound on a particular string on the violin I could associate that sound with color...
>
> If I play a B flat on the G string, I would say that the color for me is probably deep forest green. And if I play an A on the E string, that would be red. If I play the next B, if I look at it right now I would say that it's yellow. The bright colors are the upper strings of the violin -- for me I associate it with bright colors of the spectrum.
>
> Besides colors I see shapes. Each note has a shape. I would say that if you play a D on the G string, for me that's round. But if you play an A on an E string for me, that's much more flat, the shape of it. I hope not the intonation, but the shape of it.[60]

After much suffering, ultimately, many artists will come face to face with the final question of suicide if they are being wholly truthful with themself, at least at some point in their lifetime. If suffering is unbearable, and happiness is fleeting, would suicide be the only correct, and moral, path forward? As Nietzsche said, "The thought of suicide is a great consolation: by means of it one gets through many a dark night."[61] Some have given in to this particular dragon, including Van Gogh, Sylvia Plath, Cobain, David Foster Wallace, and recently poet/musician David Berman. And who is to separate these suicides from the many overdoses of the last 50 years, as we mourn so many artists now gone?

But we talk about suicide to also talk about how many artists have faced the dragon, walked through the valley, and have come back out to strengthen us. Nietzsche ultimately saw art as part of the solution to the question of suicide, a similar view as Frankl, that meaning can be found in a soul made uplifted by, "Work, love, art, and knowledge."[61]

One person who thought deeply on the question of suicide is French-Algerian philosopher Albert Camus in his first major essay *The Myth of Sisyphus* from 1942,

> There is but one truly serious philosophical problem, and that is suicide. Judging whether life is or is not worth living amounts to answering the fundamental question of philosophy. All the rest - whether or not the world has three dimensions, whether the mind has nine or twelve categories - comes afterwards. These are games; one must first answer. And if it is true, as Nietzsche claims, that a philosopher, to deserve our respect, must preach by example, you can appreciate the importance of that reply, for it will precede the definitive act. These are facts the heart can feel; yet they call for careful study before they become clear to the intellect.[62]

Camus lived through much suffering by the time he contemplated suicide at the age of 29, including overcoming tuberculosis and falling in love with a morphine-addict who ultimately was unfaithful. He found himself overcome with the sheer 'absurdity' and meaninglessness of life. But through contemplation on suffering and absurdity, and meditating on the Greek myth of Sisyphus, he found that he could understand how each life could have meaning in itself.

Sisyphus was cursed by the gods to push a rock up a mountain, and at the end of every day the rock would roll back down the mountain to be pushed up again the next. Sisyphus was always striving, never achieving. But Camus realized that the only reason we imagine Sisyphus unhappy is because we are conscious. We are always laboring in light of the goal of our labor. Otherwise, like all birds and trees and animals, we too push along the rock of existence, never reaching any final goal, always in the present moment, always pushing forward into life. So Camus realized that while we are always striving and never arriving, there could also be joy in pushing one's rock, committing yourself to the work. And ultimately he felt that this is what life is about. He concludes the essay with,

> I leave Sisyphus at the foot of the mountain! One always finds one's burden again. But Sisyphus teaches the higher fidelity that negates the gods and raises rocks. He too concludes that all is well. This universe henceforth without a master seems to him neither sterile nor futile. Each atom of that stone, each mineral flake of that night filled mountain, in itself forms a world. The struggle itself toward the heights is enough to fill a man's heart. One must imagine Sisyphus happy.

Camus sought out solitude, to work through these dragons rising up within him. As Camus wrote in his essay *The Minotaur*, "In order to understand the world, one has to turn away from it on occasions."[62] In like way solitude has been a refuge of many artists, from Jackson Pollock to Walt Whitman and Bon Iver. Within solitude the soul has space and time to slowly arise. As Swedish director Ingmar Bergman wrote in *Images: My Life in Film*,

> Here, in my solitude, I have the feeling that I contain too much humanity. It oozes out of me like a broken tube of toothpaste; it doesn't want to stay within the confines of my body. A strange feeling of weight and volume. Soul volume perhaps, which rises like clouds of smoke and envelops my body."[63]

Sequestered, the artist looks inward. Often, before an intense time of creation, there will be a more intense time of incubation. Going deep before going out. In the words of British writer Aldous Huxley, "The more powerful and original a mind, the more it will incline towards the religion of solitude."[64] Similarly, the more powerful and original an idea, the more it will require a religion of solitude to create it. This is the nature of the world, anything worth creating is hard to create, and takes time to ideate. Abba Moses, a 'desert father' and one of the early aesthetic monks in Egypt during the 300s AD, put it this way, "The man who flees and lives in solitude is like a bunch of grapes ripened by the sun, but he who remains amongst men is like an unripe grape."[65]

Within each of us is a tremendous mystery, a mystery of a soul that exists within a mortal body. There are many parts of ourself we do not really yet know or understand, and there are parts we can never fully know. The parts of us that we suppress for the sake of society and family are what psychologists like Carl Jung have called our shadow side. It strains against us, and can emerge in bitterness, anger, resentment, fury. But also subterfuge and trickery.

Carl Jung was a protege of Freud, but departed from Freud on the primacy of sexuality, and the value of transcendent experiences. Jung saw the unconscious as containing tremendous primal power if we can bring it into ourself, integrate the shadow, and use its power for good. But likewise, the shadow contains tremendous potential for damage if not contained.

To Jung, the goal was to dissolve the barriers and integrate the self,

> Unfortunately there can be no doubt that man is, on the whole, less good than he imagines himself or wants to be. Everyone carries a shadow, and the less it is embodied in the individual's conscious life, the blacker and denser it is. At all counts, it forms an unconscious snag, thwarting our most well-meant intentions.
>
> Filling the conscious mind with ideal conceptions is a characteristic of Western theosophy, but not the confrontation

> with the shadow and the world of darkness. One does not become enlightened by imagining figures of light, but by making the darkness conscious.
>
> The meeting with oneself is, at first, the meeting with one's own shadow. The shadow is a tight passage, a narrow door, whose painful constriction no one is spared who goes down to the deep well. But one must learn to know oneself in order to know who one is.[66]

What Jung said rings true, the shadow often forms a passage, a doorway, through which artists much pass to unleash their unconscious. Between them and full emotional clarity is the shadow. The unknown. Becoming a master artist means traversing the valley and learning to integrate the shadow.

Julia Cameron began teaching classes for 'blocked' creatives in New York City in the late 70s, and eventually compiled these lessons into *The Artist's Way* in 1992. This book is an incredibly valuable resource for the modern artist seeking practical methods to become more creative. One of the most useful concepts that she asks students to assume is that creativity comes from something outside, higher than oneself, a transcendent origin. So unblocking is simply removing those ways of thinking and acting that have prevented you from tapping into this powerful flow that is always there and will never leave. She sees blocks as often a result of self-sabotaging, from *The Artist's Way*,

> Most of the time when we are blocked in an area of our life, it is because we feel safer that way. We may not be happy, but at least we know what we are - unhappy. Much fear of our own creativity is fear of the unknown.
>
> If I am fully creative, what will it mean? What will happen to me and to others? We have some pretty awful notions about what *could* happen. So, rather than find out, we decide to stay blocked. This is seldom a conscious decision. It is more often an unconscious response to internalized negative beliefs.[31]

Conceptualizing the source of the creativity as coming from outside of yourself is a key part of her method. She writes,

> It is my experience both as an artist and as a teacher that when we move out on faith into the act of creation, the universe is able to advance. It is a little like opening the gate at the top of a field irrigation system. Once we remove the blocks, the flow moves in.
>
> Again I do not ask you to believe this. In order for this creative emergence to happen, you don't have to believe in God. I simply ask you to observe and note this process as it unfolds. In effect, you will be midwiving and witness your own creative progression.
>
> Creativity is an experience - to my eye a spiritual experience. It does not matter which way you think of it: creativity leading to spirituality or spirituality leading to creativity.[31]

Her perspective is that each of us has equal access to the source of creativity. We each have imbued potential to create, flowing out from within. Even if not believing this, one can benefit from behaving as if it is real. Her method works, get the book.

Along with the urge to create is the urge for a cave, a place to relax the mind to prepare the ground for creativity to emerge. Financially successful artists usually end up drawn to locations of natural beauty. Nature has an interweaving complex rhythm which relaxes the mind and draws us into the present moment. It calls to the primal part of ourself. There is beauty in the complexity of light filtering through leaves, or reflected by a million grains of sand. Transcendent beauty. There is also beauty in the complexity of anything made by human hand. We see well-crafted artistic expression as beautiful because it embodies the profound presence and life of the artist. That life is complex.

THE MYTHOLOGY OF THE ARTIST

Artists have an urge to surround themselves with beautiful artistic objects, both natural and handmade. Ancient cave paintings of powerful animals are found in the most resonant parts of caves, where bodies would gather to create collective art and ritual, immersed in and reflected by rock, surrounded by handmade beauty. Fire was certainly there, and the feeling of real fire warming our body connects us to the primal, immediately relaxing, a feeling that can bring one into the present. Imagine a collective of human bodies, moving in resonance, surrounding a fire, in the most resonant part of a cave, wall paintings in firelight. That is a primal, transcendent sensation. A collective unselfing.

What is beautiful? The artist must always keep at the forefront of the mind that beauty is a determination made by the human senses, and will always be tied to primal human needs and sensations. As Dennis Dutton illustrates in *The Art Instinct* - a path through an arching forest, the same foundational sensation of light filtering through an arching cathedral, means shelter, protection, and human habitation.[67] A well-trodden path means many humans have passed that way before, which brings a feeling of harmony, security, and beauty when represented in art. Beauty appears to be for the most part universal across cultures in fundamental ways. Philosophers have debated the meaning of beauty for thousands of years, but we also know beauty can't be fully expressed in words. Beauty is an experience, that experience is ineffable. The experience has something to do with harmony.

Beautiful sound tends to happen when all reflected surfaces are natural - wood, stone, metal, these are the sounds of human safety and habitation. Our human ear is biologically adapted to understand and interact with those surfaces. Plastic, vinyl, and other synthetic surfaces reflect sound in a way that does not sound beautiful. They sound, in a word, artificial, absorbing certain frequencies and altering the high end in a way that sounds unnaturally smothered. Just surrounding yourself with natural materials will immediately have an impact on your mental state, because of the beauty of the sightline and the reflected sound traveling back to you.

Beauty is divinely superfluous, and it calls our psyche to something greater than mere survival, in a collective capacity. Inside the stone, within the wood, humans found safety, and within this space music and art arose. Back to wood, back to stone, back to forest, back to cave. This is the primal urge of the artist, because art is known to emerge in those spaces. Beauty calls us into the present moment, it overwhelms our sensation and quiets our mind. Beauty creates an existential feeling of harmony.

The artist creates a space, a metaphorical cabin in the woods surrounded by beauty, and within this space the rational mind can become quiet. This is a prerequisite to creating art from the soul. The unconscious is like a womb, secure, within the cave surrounded by beauty where all things are provided. But within it is also tremendous power to create worlds, shape, destroy, and create again. Within it the artist is both powerful and provided for. The artist feels the pull and wants to stay, too long sometimes. Like a sleeper who never wakes, always dreaming in the opium den of the psyche. In control of all things, able to just determine to write no period at the end of a paragraph

The musician's ultimate goal is transcendence. Musicians are always chasing an ephemeral transcendence that spontaneously can descend upon the player and the listener. The chase for transcendence has justified many a self-destruction by substance abuse, from Coltrane and Bill Evans to Jim Morrison. But if beauty is a building block of transcendence, and beauty is achieved through complex harmony, then the artist's best path to transcendence is self-discipline to the craft in order to enable those complex creations. Without the knowledge of the craft the knowledge of the self is limited in expression. There will forever be a ceiling on the transcending the artist can accomplish.

That is why the path through drug use was always a lie, because more often than not it set artists on a self-destructive path that corroded their craft and left them clinging to their talent with no power or confidence. When we study the stories of music history to date we see that this path ends in destruction, of both the artist and the potential art. The path through drugs was also obscuring to the psyche, and if expressing the psyche is the goal then obscuring cannot be the method. Substances can be a tool to quiet the mind and open the psyche, but must be handled with care. Not as a shortcut to self-knowledge. And not a place for an artist to stay. Throughout history humans have used substances in ritualistic ceremonies. This constrains the abuse of the substance, and also preserves its power.

Stepping back from the 'rock star' mythology, the whole fallacy in this line of thinking is that the only path to transcendence was through inebriation. But this is only true if you can't make the ego step out of the way, so you must inebriate yourself. The compromise is you get inebriated quality of craft. In reality, transcendence is most likely to flow out of self-knowledge gained over time expressed through craft, subjugating the ego through will.

A 2017 literature review called *The Varieties of Self-Transcendent Experiences*, led by David Yaden from the University of Pennsylvania, looked at experiences the authors considered transcendent - mindfulness, awe, mystical experiences, peak experiences, and creative flow. They reviewed examples of these kind of experiences across all cultures and time, including recent surveys that found one third of respondents reporting some kind of intensely unifying experience. Art, religion, nature, romance, and even scientific logic could cause this experience. They also note the apparent overlap between mystical experiences and psychotic disorders and how these can be intertwined,

> These temporary mental states are proposed to be experienced along a spectrum of intensity that ranges from the routine (e.g., losing yourself in music or a book), to the intense and potentially transformative (e.g., feeling connected to everything and everyone), to states in between, like those experienced by many people while meditating or when feeling awe.
>
> In each account, an aspect of consciousness usually taken for granted—the sense of being a bounded, separate self—is conspicuously absent.

They conclude with a strong statement of discovery,

> ..our review suggests that Self-Transcendent Experiences are more often associated with positive outcomes such as well-being and prosocial behavior—and more intense Self-Transcendent Experiences are sometimes counted among life's most meaningful moments. We propose that a qualified consensus has emerged that, on the whole, [Sigmund] Freud was wrong and [William] James was right regarding the positive psychological potential of Self-Transcendent Experiences.[68]

From our modern viewpoint, James appears to be right and Freud wrong. Freud saw religion as an illusion, a projection of the father complex, and he saw transcendent experiences as a regression to the oceanic womb, which was negative and not in line with good mental health.

William James had a different view. He was a philosopher and America's first great psychologist, and he saw religious and transcendent experiences as essential to living a fulfilled life. Towards the end of his life he began to focus on researching what he called 'mystical experiences', which he compiled into *The Varieties of Religious Experience* in 1903. James saw two qualities that characterized a mystical experience:

1) Ineffable, meaning no adequate report of its contents can be given in words...its quality must be directly experienced; it cannot be imparted or transferred to others.

2) Noetic, meaning they are states of knowledge. They are states of insight into depths of truth unplumbed by the discursive intellect. They are illuminations, revelations, full of significance and importance, all inarticulate though they remain; and as a rule they carry with them a curious sense of authority for after-time.[69]

To summarize, a mystical experience is beyond human words and brings knowledge that illuminates the mind. It wraps you up in the present moment and overwhelms your senses. The world goes quiet, the self is transcended, and the mind is opened with awe and wonder. Suffering and transcendence feel like two sides of the same coin. The more we suffer, the more we long to transcend.

Mark Rothko was a Russian Jew who emigrated with his family to America in 1913, at the age of ten. Inspired by mythology and primitive art, he developed a painting style using only fields, or forms, of contrasting vivid color, which he felt best abstracted human emotions that create mystic experiences,

> I'm interested only in expressing basic human emotions - tragedy, ecstasy, doom, and so on - and the fact that lots of people break down and cry when confronted with my pictures shows that I communicate those basic human emotions…The people who weep before my pictures are having the same religious experience I had when I painted them. And if you, as you say, are moved only by their color relationships, then you miss the point![70]

If creation in many mythologies begins with a garden, then so those artists who are in a beautiful Eden-like space may be more likely to partake in creation. An Eden where creative things are likely to emerge, if they are bubbling beneath the surface. Only when in the garden, subjugating selfish impulses to domination, fear, anger, rage, envy, jealousy, bitterness. Once the self can be put at peace, this is a condition where peak experiences are more likely to occur, and creativity can emerge.

Although it may feel selfish, creating an Eden from time to time is justified over the life of the artist. There is a time for everything, including to go into the cocoon. Surround yourself with beauty. Surround yourself with nature. Seek after transcendence.

MUSIC AND THE BODY

All art can affect us, but music is alone in the arts in that it can physically move the body. All artists must understand music, it is elemental to all art, because it is elemental to the human body. Sound waves move the air in spherical patterns that are like Saturn's rings, gigantic ripples of air pressure undulating towards us. These pressure waves intersect with the body and eardrums, directly causing bodily sensations and emotions that can bypass the mind and enter our soul.

Within the ear is an
eardrum (tympanic membrane),
which physically moves a series of **bones** (malleus, incus, stapes),
which then moves another **membrane** (oval window),
which creates ripples in a **fluid-filled semicircular tunnel** (cochlea),
which movement is picked up by **hypersensitive hairs** (auditory cells).

That complex mechanical system is there to convert sound pressure waves into electrical signals, which can then be fed in and processed by the brain. So energy goes from air, to membrane, to bones, to membrane, to fluid, to hair, and finally to electrical signal. Direct pressure from the air, mediated through these mechanical body organs, then into brain signal, then out of the body to another body. Truly an astounding system, and what's interesting is how much mechanics are involved - stretched skin, bones, hair, fluid, all of this for us to hear anything.

Music at its most powerful is like mainlining art into the vein of the body. That is why music is a fundamental component of more complex forms of art like film. Film uses music to inject emotion directly into the body, while an interweaving storyline resonates the thoughts of the brain. Profound impact comes from art that can resonate at multiple levels of soul, body, and mind, and music can be a key.

With the advent of digital (and thus visual) audio recording came a wrong turn away from using the impact on the ears and the body as the primary decision-making factor. Young engineers relied on their eyes, sucked into the brightly colored monitor, with waveforms and graphs, without going deep into ear-training first. We produced technically perfect rhythms constructed to the grid, polished to perfection. But music is only about listening, and we react most strongly to the sound of other human bodies making human music. Human music is alive with complexity and emotion. This wrong turn included the overuse of auto-tune, digitally stripping human voices of dissonance to achieve some perfectly tuned ideal. But these dissonances, under control, are truly what attract the ear because we recognize and resonate with what is human, meaning soul expressed through body as soundwaves unfolding through time. We can't blame these young digital pioneering engineers, the sudden explosion of technology left many of them trying to figure everything out on their own without much to learn from. And so now a new generation of young engineers reaches back, into the 60s and 70s, to recreate that truly special gear and use it to make something new. To find those creative recording techniques and revive them.

Digital technology appears to be a phenomenal storage device, compared to tape - as illustrated by recent warehouse fires of original master tape recordings, some of which were lost forever. Digital as a storage device is cheap, extremely transparent, and can allow endless layer upon layer of sound. Layering moments as if they were glaze on a carefully crafted clay work of art, emotion can be made more heightened and complex by this glazing type of process. Digital is also becoming highly mobile, which will enable further recording of special situations and special environments, special moments of the soul aligning with the body in craft. Instead of using digital technology to achieve some kind of inhuman perfection, digital technology of the future will be used to capture and represent the complexity of the human condition in all of its glory and struggle.

Much of our music in America was born out of suffering. The blues were born out of suffering, from deep within the body over time, and dissonance is part of what makes that sound so engaging. Similarly, Celtic and bluegrass music uses dissonance to create a sense of brooding tragedy over time, born out of suffering. Both singing styles are a deep groaning from the depths of the body, the body muscles relaxed as if by exhaustion, with the diaphragm fully engaged. These emotions arise out of life's struggle and that sound is a fundamental one that can resonate the soul. I hear a weary voice mourning and I am stirred with that emotion.

We must freely express, especially in dark times, the sense of suffering that is the dissonance of the human voice. We must ultimately tune our instruments and voice by ear, and let the human ear instruct us in how much dissonance provokes beauty and complexity in the soul. As suffering increases, more dissonance might be required to express it musically. Digital technology can allow complex layering of dissonant and consonant sounds and textures, as well as layering of various spaces on one another, which can create something new. But it must always submit to the human ear, body, soul.

Music in its most primal form is just human bodies in the most resonant part of a cave, or in the wooden house, resonating the unconscious together with sound. That is why a movement is needed away from the musician on the stage, a performer for the consumer, forever being consumed. We must turn back to the bodies in the woods, in the cave, resonating together. No separation and no hierarchy, music must become more primal, collective, and ritualistic. Back to collective resonation. These resonations can tune our psyche to move in more healthy collective ways. Similar to how a hive has an efficiently uniform way of thinking, we can resonate rhythmically together for any collective purpose we determine is worth the effort. A glance through history shows what humans are able to accomplish when in collective resonation. We have that creative capability at our command endlessly by simply being a human with a soul.

Musicians like Ray Charles and the Staples Singers took music directly lifted from the gospel context and placed it into a secular context and received the same emotional result. Bob Marley did the same with reggae, incorporating the spiritually transcendent aspects of Rastafari practices. This fluidity of music from religious to secular spheres shows that popular art pulls at the same basic impulse for deep expression and emotional transcendence that are expressed through religious rituals. These musicians saw how religious music impacted the body and just lifted that into another sphere.

Bodies move a certain way, and when we hear music from those bodies our bodies impact with those soundwaves and resonate in time. We receive music in our body in relation to our own body's rhythm - is it the pace of our running body? Walking? Working? We feel the emotional weight of its movement, how it is in front of or trailing a beat, relaxed or pushed. How it falls. Watch any great musician and you will see a whole body in service to a rhythm, moving within its tempo. Our bodies respond to that movement, which is what constitutes a great piece of music. But then lyrics, melody, and harmony can layer on a complexity to the bodily emotion, and start to resonate at different levels between body, mind and soul. This resonance is immersing, and pulls the participants into the moment.

Master musicians will play with the rhythm in complex ways, expressing subtlety of emotion beyond the imagination of a beginner. A breadth of education is available to the modern musician by simply studying the music of other cultures. The past twenty years, a blink of human history, has opened up a world of music (and all forms of art) that humans have never had access to. Fifty years ago not even the wealthiest person had immediate access to all of the music in the world, something most people have on their phone today.

The music we hear from each culture is the result of a long process of interaction over time between the soul and body. The Cuban Buena Vista Social Club shows how one can relax into the beat with the body, pulling up slightly behind it, whereas the tight funk of New Orleans' The Meters snaps behind the beat like a string on a bow. The slow pocket of Miles Davis's Kind of Blue created a languorous modal mood that envelopes the body with weight. Each interaction creates emotions. Each of these arises naturally out of the bodies of these performers and originators, they played them in the funky and original way their bodies moved.

The modern master musician must make use of all of these sources of influence and pull them into the soul, to re-emerge in something completely unique and new for this time and place. It will be both new and very old. A reach forward by combining primal expressions of emotion into a new thing. In the same way, the music of a master musician could come from no other. The tone and emotion are entirely unique, as each artist is a unique soul and body with its own mythology. The master artist pushes further into that uniqueness over time. Eventually what appears plain and simple will become deep as the artist deepens.

Modern western music is built upon what was basically a compromise to push all of the audible tones into twelve equally-spaced notes that easily lent itself to the newly invented piano. This happened relatively recently, in the 1500s. Other scales that existed at the time had more or less tones than this, the Arab Tone System had 24 tones. So it was clear that more tones existed than these twelve. The twelve-tone scale was a compromise that allowed 'equal temperament', meaning the notes could harmonize well with one another in a predictable way and could be laid out on a piano in octaves. And thus the foundation was laid for the rich outpouring of western harmony-based music, from Bach to Mozart to Mahler to Oscar Robertson to Patsy Cline to the Pixies. The foundation of all western music, that has now conquered the world, is based on this compromise. The compromise was certainly worth it, as so many instruments could simply tune to the piano and everything was pretty much in tune from there. However, the compromise left behind many tones that are simply not represented in western music.

Many of the oldest forms of music are what we call monophonic. They have a single flying melody, usually over a bed of some kind of drone type of texture. This is the sound of the ringing voice or instrument, a single traveler, the main character taking a journey. It's really the core component sound of a story and a very old form of music. A single hero on a journey over time, through valleys and over mountains.

Most of the classical music of the eastern world is monophonic and storylike in this way. Classical Indian music has the beautiful drone of the tanpura as the backdrop. The tanpura forms a misty wind, it sounds dark, alive, and brooding. Then the sitar main character journeys out, slowly, taking the first steps and breathing in the day like a little child about to play in the dirt. It dances around and forms little motifs that are picked up later, played with, turned around, flipped upside down, and then dropped. The tablas join in to play, back and forth, with the sitar. There are variations but this is the general structure across many cultures of the Middle East and Asia. And this appeared to be the case in some early European music. The music of the monks is monophonic, against a drone, as are many of the early Gregorian chants and other liturgical music, as is much of the old Celtic music. It is often deep sounding and monophonic, like a slow men's choir.

In the 60s, western popular music became, for a few years, very infatuated with the Indian tanpura and drone music, including The Velvet Underground, John Cale, and The Beatles. But before that in America there was La Monte Young, a radical free-thinking musician who built mechanical instruments that would drone like the 60 hz hum of American electricity. From his 2002 interview with *American Public Media*,

> The other sound that really had a big influence on me was the sound of step-down transformers on telephone poles in an electrical yard. I would ask my mother, "What is the wind?" I was very curious, and I would talk about the wind at ages as early as 2 or 3 years old. Looking out the window and seeing it move the alfalfa that was growing outside the cabin, my mother would try to explain to me what the wind was. But while she was talking, I was also listening to the sound of these telephone poles, and it was just a continuous steady hum. This continuous steady hum is the ancestral origin of my work with sixty-cycles, which is the frequency that the electrical companies provide the power to us in the United States: 60 cycles per second. Everywhere we go, we hear this 60 cycle drone

and, or, other frequency components that are related to this drone. Eventually I began to tune all of my music that I do in the U.S. with electronics to this 60 cycle per second drone, because even in today's year, 2001-2002, and even with the best equipment, there is still some residual hum. (60 cycles per second.) If you create music that is in tune with this hum, then there can never be an interference with the music that you are creating. It's the idea that it is the strongest drone in our vicinity.[71]

La Monte Young felt that drones represented a universal consciousness, and that their 'periodicity' evoked something primal within our own biology. Listening to his composition *The Tortoise, His Dream and Journeys*, it is just one long moving journey around a single note, in and out with thick metallic resonance, produced by some mechanical hum generator.[71] The tones interweave in cycles. Moving in and out of sync, cycling. As we tune to the interweaving wavelengths we are pulled into the moment.

Drones are some of the earliest known instruments. Drone instruments are a fundamental part of ancient music from the Near East and Southeast Asia, and eventually made their way into Europe. We know the ancient Celts used drones in battle, fierce horse-head waspy drones, held up high and played by blowing air up through like a giant raspy trumpet. A whole formation of these would lead the troops in battle like a deafening angry swarming hive of bees. This later incarnated into the more civilized bagpipes. Another ancient drone instrument from Europe was the hurdy-gurdy, basically two strings played in a circular loop by hand-crank. It sounds like a boxy tanpura, a western take on an eastern sound.

The Indian tanpura is the quintessential drone instrument - it looks like a large gourd, with four strings which are designed to produce mostly harmonics, which is just the overtones. The four strings are plucked one at a time in a cycle, and the oscillations from the conflicting harmonic overtones produce a constant cycling of tones, over and under. The tones cycle around a home, or 'tonic' note. It sounds like moving coils of metal are coming into and out of alignment. The tempo is slow, like a mother rocking a child. Then, when an instrument solos on top of that, it moves - farther from the tonic with greater dissonance, closer to the tonic with more pleasant consonance, always ultimately resolving to the relaxing home base of the tonic. An interesting study from 2017 led by Dipak Gosh looked at brain waves of subjects while listening to the Indian tanpura drone. What they found was that the alpha and theta waves measured from the temporal lobe increased in 'complexity', basically became more dense and active and alive, while listening to tanpura drone. Just listening to recordings of the tanpura drone increased activity of alpha and theta waves in the temporal lobe of participants on the study.[72]

This is a fascinating connection between sound waves and brain waves. Alpha brain waves oscillate at around 8 to 12 cycles per second, which is 8-12 hz. These brain waves have been associated with creative thought, relaxed wakefulness, and a pleasant floating feeling. Right before you fall asleep you are likely to have an increase in alpha brainwaves. Recent research out of UNC Chapel Hill found that creativity could be increased in human subjects by administering a 10 hz wave of electricity to the frontal cortex.[73] It's so unexpected to me that they could induce creativity by a targeted wave of electricity cycling at a certain rate. The connection between alpha brain waves and creativity is a very interesting one that we don't completely understand.

Theta brain waves are slower at 4 to 7 cycles per second (hz) and are associated with the first stage of sleep. In theta state you have just slipped out of consciousness, into the dream world. This is the hypnagogic, or dreamlike state, with borderline or partial awareness, imagery, reverie, and drowsiness. In this state researchers say people are highly suggestive.

Thomas Budzynski was a psychologist who spent his whole life chasing theta brain waves. He was a member of the 1960s "biofeedback" cohort of psychologists who attempted to use new scientific therapy methods to solve psychological problems. Budzynski would hook his patients up to EEG machines and guide them into the realm of theta waves, as indicated on the EEG that he was reading in realtime. The goal was to guide the patient into what he called 'twilight learning'. As he wrote in 1977 in Psychology Today,

> For a brief time as we lie in bed at night, neither fully awake nor yet asleep, we pass through a twilight mental zone that Arthur Koestler has described as a state of reverie. Many people associate this drowsy stage with hallucinatory images, more fleeting and disjointed than dreams, and compare it to the viewing of a speeded-up, jerky series of photographic slides. A host of artists and scientists have credited the imagery of this twilight state with creative solutions and inspiration for their work.
>
> ..we are now beginning to understand that during this brief somnolent state, people not only may have creative insights but may also be more in touch with the unconscious in general.[74]

So the music of the Indian tanpura drone provokes alpha and theta brain waves, which could lead us into a dreamlike twilight state, with creative daydreaming. It is very interesting that this most ancient form of music has such a tremendous impact on the brain, and on particular brain waves. Did ancient humans develop this music to induce these altered states? It speaks to the collective origination of music - they gathered, to the sound of the drone, maybe joining their voices into the drone as they enter the circle, and their brainwaves respond and sync together. It does feel that in many of these ancient forms of music the drone sets the headspace and the melody tells the story, the drone sets the velvet backdrop and the melody paints the movement. And still now this ancient music holds great power.

Over time music developed and complexity emerged. Complexity naturally increases in human culture as time progresses, it is the result of a new branch of culture breaking out and then being layered on, in waves, periodic waves of culture over the generations. That complexity in music is beautiful to the ear. In my opinion this is because when we hear musical complexity it represents the intense complexity of our lives. We feel the stories merging and intertwining, and we learn something about ourselves and about time, and we feel amazement, awe, joy, and meaning in that moment. We learn something about how we relate to society, about our place in the hive. We can have an epiphany just listening to a complexly beautiful piece of music. Gregorian chant music flowed out of social complexity, as you can obviously hear because it sounds like many deep voices droning together. It seems we are able to feel cathartic in that human complexity. We identify with it.

An interesting case study in the development of modern music is the folk music from the country of Georgia, near Eastern Europe. This is as described by Tsurtsumia and Jordania In *Echoes from Georgia: Seventeen Arguments on Georgian Polyphony (2010)*.[75] I happened upon this excellent book because I was trying to find information on Eastern European music, in particular the incredibly beautiful harmonies I heard on a documentary called *Sufi Soul*.[41] In that documentary William Daryrymple goes to a sacred music festival and a group singing this very haunting music appears briefly on screen, dressed in white clothing fringed with colored cotton designs. The harmonies were layered and highly complex, like a bluegrass choir, circling through major and minor chords and even in-between. I figured based on the chords that they must be Eastern European. After searching for a while I found a chapter from this book, which led me to some incredible videos of these traditional peoples singing.

This book describes how, in the mountains of Georgia, there appears to have been a departure from the monophonic style that dominated the rest of the world. The Svans of North Georgia began to create what is some of the earliest European polyphony, with multiple tones at once. They live at over 3,000 meters elevation, and still speak the ancient Svan language, up in the rugged mountains, preserving this culture and music. These people live at a crossroads of east and west, bordered by Iran, Turkey, and Russia, so they built on these musical influences and created their own kind of music.

Listening to Svanetian music to me feels like going back in time and hearing monophony plus. The drone is still there, but the melody is sung by groups of men together, they jostle with each other moving from consonance to dissonance over different tones. Then they speed up and clap together. It feels intense, deep in the body, it is also overwhelming to hear, like trying to run barefoot through a rushing river. Quite powerful, with multiple streams interweaving. These deep jostling tones rumble through your body moving in and out of harmony, and most of the lead is in the range of baritone vocals. It's fundamentally monophonic, but with dark moving shades of harmony.

The next development was the music in neighboring Kakheti. They are down in the valley and it is a beautiful sunny region where wine grapes are grown and tourists would go to vacation. So they were naturally slightly wealthier, and had a very social drinking culture. They developed 'table songs' that flowed out of summertime banquets where hosts would sing these songs to serenade guests. These table songs became highly complex, because they took the harmonious drone of the Svans and then added onto it a soaring monophonic lead character. It is like as soon as the west developed the beginnings of a polyphonic sound, the next town over merged it with the best of the east and came up with something amazing. A surging lead over a rushing polyphony. Fitting the geography and people, these songs are more relaxed and happy sounding. And here we see the human story, people up in the mountains and down in the valleys, pushing and shaping the craft to embody their region. Humans being humans, resilient and innovative and expressive. The table songs were sung by men and women over a chorus of harmony, depending on the song.

To me the Kakhetian music sounds like a close relative putting an arm around you, telling you life is rough but everything is going to be OK. The music has a beautiful movement over time, going into valleys of deep dissonance, and then upward into beautiful hills. There is a drone of vocal tones that ripple underneath. It still has a deep rumbly sound but there is sweetness of harmony, more major chords, and bits of beauty at times as the lead dives in and out. Beauty pops out occasionally, not constantly, and there is also moments that sound quite sorrowful. We feel the lead is being consumed by darkness and pain, but then back up again into a hopeful sound. The overall impression leaves one feeling ruddy and resilient and sturdy. It seems that because dissonance expresses pain so well, complicated dissonance into consonance is what provokes our soul, because we see ourselves in it. We know we are dissonant and we long to be consonant, so it expresses something deep about our story over time. Our soul becomes the lead character, and with it we go down into suffering and come out again victorious. Transcendent music shows us the quest as we follow it with our soul.

The later development in this progression was in Kutaisi, which is the third biggest city in Georgia and a hub of culture. The sound of Kutaisi has more fifths and more major chord harmony, very smooth and packaged and statuesque and even more organized and complex, but in a way that was quite manicured compared to the rough Kakhetian sound. To me this sound is over-polished, but I can see the attraction and it seems to have been the most influential. Fifths and polished major chords were favorites of the big classical composers. It communicated the divine authority perhaps. But they never quite mastered the movement from dissonance to consonance, and major to minor, like Kakhetian music. That is what communicates the human to me. These singers are not confined to the twelve tone scale, they are just fluidly moving as the human voice moves, in and between our western tones. And so they can mine deeper levels of movement between dissonance and consonance, the whole world in between, the grey areas of complexity. That complexity is cathartic, and beautiful to our ears. To my ears, it's even more cathartic than Bach or Mozart. Beethoven's *Ninth* does get to me so I do put some classical pieces on par. But from my point of view I feel I need that twisting from major to minor, consonance to dissonance, to really feel that catharsis.

So we see a different kind of musical emotion emerging out of different geographies, which produced different kinds of people (and/or attract certain kinds of people), who came together to sing out of their souls and out of their culture. The culture just naturally emerged from their outward motion, and so we must now push outward and we can also create new culture. The culture pushes out with art and music and, hopefully, the best of what is old will merge with the best of what is new. This is what humans do when they move forward, this is what human society naturally does when at its best.

Another interesting look at musical geography is in Africa. From the north, the Islamic countries, comes monophonic (single lead) minor key (mournful sounding) music. In countries like Morocco the monophony is mournful but also incredibly lively. The sound of driving life, with sorrow, together, on a journey. The tone is sad but resilient. The time signatures are blocky, but the rhythm fits the body, so it feels like a pleasant jerking back and forth, over and under, the journey moves along. Moroccan music has complex layering of shakers and tambourines and hand drums, a percussive bed that is almost like a drone, a hand drum drone. Then from neighboring Libya comes drones and monophonic chants, but there is more call and response, with a relaxed swing of the body. Egyptian traditional music feels more upbeat and rigid, like bodies in a line dancing together, with hand drums and call and response. Angola also has call and response but with large hand drums and shouting, neither major nor minor sounding, somewhere in between. Down farther south it takes more of a turn towards the major, Cameroon has call and response in a joyful laid-back rhythm, it sounds like the celebration after a hunt. South Africa has famous call and response in major chorus choir, like the lion king, masterful gigantic sounds, walls of people with authority and power underneath. As we look across Africa the continent's music goes from minor to major, sad expressiveness to happy expressiveness, but all with a very rhythmic basis, always connected to the body. In these cultures music is never divorced from dance, music is the outflow of bodies in dance, the two are one, and the rhythms are made for the body. It's almost as if major and minor, happy and sorrowful, were a seasoning developed over time - the north preferred the minor flavor, the south and west preferred the major flavor, and the middle countries blended the spices together for something new.

Knowing all of this, musicians should be less afraid to venture off into tunings you can hear, but may not be able to pick up on a meter. Or rhythms you can feel, but can't count out in time. Science can never trump our human hearing, our body, because music is from and for only humans. I have found that a digital tuner can give a good starting point, for getting things close. Then quiet everything, and listen to the guitar interacting with the room. Begin playing with each note in turn, slowly, and try to align each little harmonic with each other. Connect your emotions to your fingers on the tuner, and listen to the feelings that come up. Try to listen through the notes for the resonances behind the notes, the little subharmonic resonances. If you can align all the little subharmonics to a beautiful sound, and then align that with the room, then stop, you have found it.

This should all be by ear in the end. Your ear is the same as every human ear. A beautiful sound is a beautiful sound, your body is every human body, your soul is every human soul. So trust your ear, connect to your emotions, and go with your instinct. Be in the moment and feel the dissonances shift with the tuners. Feel it go in and out of resonance, you can feel it within your body. Eventually you will start to get a feel for dissonance. It's a darkness you can work with, like clay, and it can be quite deep and rich.

Through your tuning you can push the tone towards subtleties of feeling, sometimes of sadness, sometimes of wholeness, and sometimes just a feeling like a round shape in the right place. We should not be afraid of dissonance. We should push into sounds of human flaws and complexity, layered over beauty which conveys hope. Guitarists can do this by bending strings, as the guitar neck can convey all the in-between tones if the player is clever. Jaco Pastorius was a brilliant American jazz bassist who came to prominence in the late 70s. He filed the frets off of his bass so as not be inhibited by the western twelve tones - he wanted every tonal option available. His music was uninhibited and expressive, but he lost himself in mental health problems, self-destructive tendencies, and substance abuse, dying at age 35.

Music at its most fundamental is just resonance. Guitar players listen for the resonance of the room, the string, the body, the wood of the guitar, there is even a resonance from the human body. A human holding a guitar sounds certainly different than that guitar played by a robot. The human component of that reflected sound is much of what imbues it with warmth, complexity, and emotion. It sounds intimate, because we hear the body, we hear the breath, we feel the presence, we hear the fingertips on the slightly worn bronze guitar strings. We hear these real physical human sounds and emotions, we connect, and we resonate in time. So the first thing you have to be willing to do is stop everything, be silent, and listen.

From a great listener, La Monte Young,

> ..when I sing outdoors, I listen to the resonance of the canyon or the ocean, or whatever is the natural resonance of the woods... Let's say I'm walking through the woods. I sit and listen to the resonant frequency. It's easy to hear it because the birds sing at this frequency. They tune in to the resonance of the woods. You hear different birdcalls reflecting this resonance, although the calls are different. What is a resonance? A resonance is that frequency which, if you assume that you have two parallel walls, a resonant frequency is that frequency which starts on one wall, hits the other wall, and gets back to wall number 1 just in time to reinforce the very next positive pulse of the frequency. This is resonance of the simplest type. These occur in many different kinds of situations including outdoors, in canyons and in caves, tunnels, and in the woods. So, in that kind of situation, one might choose this natural resonance that is taking place, and perform with that. In the case of electronics, the 60 cycles is really the strongest frequency that we have to deal with.
>
> It's like looking for universal constants. Eventually we're all looking for these special frequencies to which everything else is related, frequencies that have then a harmonic structure, which in turn is related to the structure of the universe.[71]

When picking with your fingers or pick, recently I've been using a metal thumbpick, there are infinite numbers of ways to hold and pick a guitar. Different body positions result in different reflected body sounds. A different angle of wrist results in a different angle of attack. Each sound is a balance between the attack, or the initial percussive part, the sustain, and the decay, or the tail. How they interact can vary tremendously, and both interact with everything in the room. You should quickly run through a huge range of volume and velocity of attacks, different body positions, different sounding decays, different types of palm-muting. All of these variations will resonate the room, strings, wood, and body differently. Play through hundreds of iterations quickly, just move fluidly through as many combinations as possible and keep your ears wide open for tone, especially if you are in a new room. This is simply a tone exercise - abstract and separate out the tone, focus, listen, think, feel, until the tone is right. Then open your eyes, look down, and try not to move. Record that emotion.

Play with each note in turn, listen to the room and how the notes interact. Pull back and try to listen from afar. In this way you can focus on the tone and abstract it - it's not a guitar anymore, just a tone, you have in your hands the first ever Tone Knobs. Shift away from left-brain digital categorical thinking, like 'you are 34.33 cents flat', and more into the language of creativity. Words of feeling instead of categories. This seems simple but these tricks we can use on ourselves are powerful. That particular trick came out of Daniel Lanois' book *Soul Mining: A Musical Life*.[76] Lanois helped produce some transcendent albums, like U2's *The Joshua Tree* and Emmy Lou Harris's *Wrecking Ball*. He was adept at changes lenses. If we need to change a lens, we can learn how to put on different lenses and blink our eyes. His trick can be universalized - change the words. Instead of EQ label it 'smooth' and 'shiny', or maybe 'red' and 'brown', or just transform the fader into a velocity arm.

Just like the guitar is mostly about resonance, so is the human voice. Singing for me has been at times a torment, and also at times a quest. Using my voice came with a lot of fear because it was so untrustworthy. But when working on the last album, after practicing one to two hours daily for several months, I came to know my voice more intimately. One thing I realized, that I would have never realized had I only practiced thirty minutes a day, is that after an hour or so my voice would loosen up and my diaphragm would connect more directly to my vocal chords. It would sound to the listener like my tone became more full and round.

Elvis, Sinatra, Orbison, these giants of singing had very open round tones of voice.

Learning to sing has been like learning to be creative, you sometimes have to try less to achieve more. And so learning to sing in the last few years has been learning to relax every muscle in my body, so that finally the diaphragm can fully engage. When every chest and back and shoulder and neck muscle is relaxed, then the large natural cavity of your chest can be filled and interact with your tone and sound beautiful. Eventually, after enough practice, I started to regain a confidence in my voice that I had lost over time, and I finally trusted I could get to that place of beautiful vocal tone whenever I needed it. Which means I relaxed more, and was able to sing better. And a virtuous cycle began. The shape of the chest is very important. The starting point should be excellent posture, with a column of air supported by the diaphragm. Once the muscles are all relaxed, then you can begin to play more with varying the shape of the resonance.

Johnny Cash was usually upright in the middle and hunched over with one shoulder, curved, to one side, which would pull deeper and rounder overtones into his voice. Similarly, Elvis would curl his upper lip to create unique overtones from the odd shaped cavity, resonating between chest and mouth. Some voices simply come out of who the person is at heart, no manipulation needed, like Odetta and Sam Cooke. Pure genuine emotion. Sam Cooke sings with the most natural, open, warm tone that exists. Chet Baker holds his mouth upward, like a trumpet, and puts a trumpeter's column of breath under every note, always in control. So each voice, at its best, would certainly sound extremely unique. The open tone, like Sam Cooke achieved, was the sound of his body, and each body is different just as each soul is different. Out of this body-soul combination comes a unique sound with emotion. Everyone should learn to sing, it is very cathartic. But mastery of singing comes out of mastery of the body, because the voice is ultimately an emanation of the body.

The history of music is a history of various streams mingling in the desert, each being transformed. Different cultures have specialized in different kinds of complexity of emotion, and then neighboring cultures borrowed from that. The 12-tone scale of Western music allowed the creation of tremendously moving walls of sound, harmony upon harmony like Beethoven's *Moonlight Sonata* or Handel's *Messiah*. Western music also had a stream out of Celtic roots, which blended with centuries of church tradition to make folk hymns and ballads. But it wasn't until these two styles of music met the expression of African-American soul that an explosion of musical styles were born. Jazz, blues, rock, rnb, soul, all of these genres of music emerged out of the fertile mixing ground that was popular western music in the 50 and 60s.

Similarly, we now have the music of all cultures at our fingertips and artists must absorb all of it, what it teaches us about the human condition, and about new ways of musical expression. We must incorporate the yearning of the Imam's cry, the blues singer's wail, the African chorus chant, and the bluegrass holler. Each shows us something unique in human emotion, something ineffable, beyond words, that's present in us. We feel that yearning in our body and our soul resonates with their emotional expression. As musicians, we are artists, we don't want to repeat what has come before, we want to press into the new. So the new must build on what has come before, it must be Nick Drake with Billie Holliday and Otis Redding. Or however it comes to be, but whatever it is it must go beyond what has come before, building on and learning from those emotions. Art from a healthy society is always layering, improving, increasing in complexity and emotional clarity.

Audio engineering is a bit of a dark art. Superstar producers in the 70s, 80s, and 90s would guard their secrets carefully, passing things on only to a few lucky apprentices. I began to learn about audio engineering out of necessity - because I wanted to record my ideas. I did my first few albums with four microphones and a simple computer interface. But as I got deeper into it I realized certain albums I loved had a sonic quality that evoked strong emotion. They just had a sound. Whole eras had a sound, different genres had iconic sounds, and these sounds would pull me into the emotion. So I began to look deeper into some of my favorite albums - the folk crooners of the 70s like James Taylor and Cat Stevens, the muscular pop of 90s alt-country like the Black Crowes and the Wallflowers, the British mojo of Radiohead. Most of these artists worked with very experienced studios and producers, on big budgets, with sometimes unlimited amounts of time to experiment. It was not uncommon for huge bands to take six months, or even a year to record an album. They would dig until a totally original sound emerged. Peter Gabriel and Daniel Lanois spent a year creating *So* in a barn in the English countryside. U2 rented a castle to record *The Unforgettable Fire*.

I read all the books accessible on audio engineering, read the forums, listened to all the interviews, and watched the documentaries. George Martin, sometimes called the sixth Beatle, was an icon to me. As was Tom Dowd from the 70s, Tchad Blake from the 90s, and Nigel Godrich in the 00s. The deeper I dug the more an interesting story began to take shape, of an industry rocked over and over by innovation, driven by fads, and ultimately vulnerable to its own flaws as it was a system built on exploitation. But just the gear itself told a very interesting story.

Originally audio was recorded onto wax cylinders, which was pressed onto shellac or later onto vinyl which became the delivery mode of choice. Tape was a huge improvement over wax once it became available in the 40s, and it brought a slow-motion revolution in recording techniques. Tape allowed much higher fidelity, but it was also easy to chop and splice, and engineers could develop a feel for how to best manipulate it. Early pioneers of tape recording, like Les Paul, experimented with overdubbing onto existing tracks to create a new 'merged' sound, which was a radical idea in the 40s. Eventually technology caught up and Ampex released the first eight track tape machine in the 50s, allowing simultaneous recording of up to eight tracks at a time. Over time recording consoles and tape machines became more complex as into the 60s multitrack recording would explode into public consciousness with the experimentation of the Beach Boys and the Beatles.

The sound of music, the power behind amplifiers for electric guitars, stereos in cars, and radios in living rooms, was all from vacuum tubes through the 1950s. These were glass tubes sealed with a gas to create a vacuum, in which a wire is heated and electrons were captured thermionically. Because an element was actually being physically heated, these vacuum tubes could get very hot, they could easily break, and they were bulky. They basically looked like large filament light bulbs. In the early 1960s solid state transistors began to replace tubes in the electronics marketplace, and these new transistor devices were much smaller with almost no heat. However, the subjective audio quality, the sound of transistors compared with tubes was lacking. The tubes sounded fuller, warmer, more 3-dimensional, more realistic. Sparkly highs, beautiful midrange, round extended lows. And today many still believe they sound best.

Rupert Neve was a British citizen who grew up in Argentina, the son of missionary parents. He was truly an electronics prodigy who began designing tube amplifiers from the age of 13. He designed and built a mobile recording studio for the British Navy at the age of 17. He then worked for hi-fi home system designers in England before starting his own Neve company in 1960. Clients were coming to him around this time and asking, can you figure out how to build transistor audio production gear that sounds as good as vacuum tubes? His first big project was an all transistor mixing desk for Phillips Recording Studio in London in 1964. It was a huge success.

He had studied tube designs and figured out that much of the beauty of the sound comes from the transformers, the components that step (or transform) the power up and down. Transformers affect the audio spectrum in special ways, saturating as they are driven by more and more power. So Neve spent a tremendous amount of time auditioning different prototypes of hand-wound transformers, with different metal materials like iron and nickel, listening with his trained ears until he found the secret combination that make Neve designs sound so rich. There is magic in his unique combination of transistors with hand-wound transformers. His sound was different than a tube sound, more creamy in texture, like hot milk poured into black coffee, and thus became extremely popular with the jazz crowd. It sounded iconic and larger than life, with a slightly reset midrange that typifies the polite 'British' preference for tone. Over time these original modules became more and more valuable, they are now in the tens of thousands of dollars for a single module, and hundreds of thousands for a mixing desk. One reason they are so hard to clone is the metal that made these transformers was mostly iron but had additional cross-contaminants laced throughout, because the tolerance for contamination of metals was higher at the time. The specialness of the metal is the complexity of natural contamination, chosen by Rupert Neve's ears. The combination of transformer and transistor cushioned the sound, rounded out the sound, smoothed out the sound, almost like a thermionic vacuum tube would do. But this was all ultimately envisioned and created by Neve.

In America a few years later, in 1968, a rival powerhouse was about to begin. API was started by Saul Walker, building on the electronics knowledge and experience he had acquired in the American Navy. He began to design audio recording consoles that utilized the operational amplifier, or op-amp for short. Op-amps are more complex than single transistors and can theoretically create a cleaner signal path, or a quite dirty sounding signal path, depending on how they are implemented. Saul's design utilized a synergy between op-amp and transformer (taking from Neve) to create a sound that had plenty of hair and mojo when run hot, but was beautifully clean in a dark shiny way when run at normal levels. He was tuning by ear for punch, and instead of iron transformers he used silicon steel. The Saul Walker API sound is punchy through and through, and the texture sounds more dry, more immediate, while punching outward into the listener. If the Neve sound is bigger than life, the API sound is a punch in the chest. The weight of the API sound is concentrated in the low-mids, with a dense cardboard kind of warmth. This sound became quit popular until eventually API, or similar op-amp configured gear, became the iconic sound of the 70s. And this was the sound I loved, and felt at home with.

Warm, close, and textured like Neil Young, Rod Stewart, Cat Stevens, and Lou Reed. My explorations came into perfect sync with the home-recording revolution's second boom, which has been clones of vintage historic gear finally becoming available to the masses. I was able to buy an older API style preamp from a company named CAPI, and put in a Melcor 70s style 1731 Op-Amp. And what I heard sounded like home. The API sound is dense, mid-forward in the American style, there is thickness and aggression but quite warm, so most of the energy is in the midrange. It's more 'forward' than the polite but creamy Neve sound. You can feel the thump of acoustic guitars, and the chesty overtones of Cat Stevens. To me these original op-amp designs seemed to bring out a dark, woody, earthy overtone to everything that runs through it.

There was another unique sound in the 60s, and that was George Martin's sound with Apple. The Beatles. George Martin was a unique character, he was a brilliant classical pianist who ended up buying a recording studio but didn't have a lot of studio experience. He began recording comedy albums with people like Peter Sellers, drawing on his creativity to get the most relaxed and unique sound performances on tape. When The Beatles came into his studio he was initially less than impressed, but agreed to help them work some songs into a record. What he found once they were in the studio is four musicians who were incredibly adept at creative experimentation. Their voices and instruments were completely at command, as they had been playing hours per night every night at strip clubs in Germany. They moved as one organism, in sync, together.

And so Martin's natural curiosity combined with the Beatles spontaneous creative playfulness and a momentous collaboration was born. Martin became famous for using large amounts of audio compression, which up to that time had mostly been a tool for ensuring audio didn't exceed volume thresholds. Martin experimented with smashing Ringo's drums hard through the classic Fairchild 660 compressor. This was a beast of a compressor designed by chaining many tube circuits together to gently round and limit volume in a natural way. Every Fairchild used 20 tubes and 11 transformers, and weighed over 60 lbs. When Martin smashed Ringo's drums through the Fairchild compressor they became larger and rounder and bigger than life, with tremendous weight and heft, and a whole new thumpy pop sound was born. Martin prefigured the heavy use of creative compression that would come to define pop.

From the 50s until the 90s, money poured into the music industry and more and more experimentation was going on in big studios with big budgets. While some engineers were playing with gear for emotional effect, there was also a way of thinking that was trying to capture music as pure as possible.

Each piece of gear left its own sonic fingerprint. Most engineers worked with analog tape on reels, the same technology used in film. Tape had its own unique sound characteristics. It was certainly not 'pure' in a technical sense. Tape has its own compression curve, it naturally pushes back against spikes in volume because loud sounds saturate tape and are cushioned as the tape overloads. Different tape machines and different tape reels overloaded in different ways, and certain tape machines, like the Revox A77 and the Studer A827, became well-known for their signature sound characteristics. Tape had a texture that sounded 'tapey', a slightly crunchy harmonic distortion that sounds very alive and dynamic. It limited volume in a very natural way. Tape also gently rolled off the highest and lowest octaves, and the roll-off of the high-end, the range of dogs and bats, was very important for the natural warmth tape is known for. Once again, different brands of tape, different tape machines, hitting the tape at different volumes, produces a range of compression, distortion, and roll-off effects. Tape also produced slight variances between the left and right channels of audio, which resulted in a pleasant chorusy effect which engineers called 'wow' and 'flutter', slight pitch and tone variations over time.

Some engineers grew weary of constantly fighting these side effects from imperfect gear. Overdubbing onto tape would build up noise over time, the natural white noise we hear in older recordings, and technologies like Dolby Noise Reduction were introduced to counteract the noise accumulation that comes from overdubbing and combining tape recorded tracks. These engineers dreamed of an audio technology free from the mechanical quirks and audible distortions of analog gear. And in the late 70s along came digital technology, which seemed to offer an answer.

As audio technology developed in the 60s and 70s, gear manufacturers would pitch their gear as having the most natural, pure, realistic sound. Microphone manufacturers developed microphones with a slight lift in the high frequencies, to overcome the natural high-end roll-off of tape. Gear designers began to aim for specs as much as sound, and 'low distortion' was a big selling point. Part of the problem is 'distortion' was a vaguely defined audio concept - it basically meant any deviation from purity. But because purity was so difficult to define, distortion became a giant catch-all term, and low distortion became a primary goal divorced from the character and quality of a sound.

Once digital came along, with theoretically no distortion, it seemed like the ideal of audio purity could finally be realized. Sound and music could finally be captured in its true light. But something happened engineers did not anticipate - all of that technically 'pure' gear, designed to work with crunchy magnetic tape and analog consoles, sounded different on digital. It sounded harsh and sterile. It was like all of this gear was designed to push against a veil, but when the veil was lifted it sounded worse.

A similar trend occurred when digital technology made its way into television in America, and this is so similar as to be quite a useful analogy. Around 2006 American television stations replaced their analog broadcast signals with digital ones, and consumers had to buy new antennas to receive the digital transmissions. Most television stations had long before switched to digital video storage, which was significantly easier and cheaper and much cleaner looking than dealing with tape. But this new digital signal, transmitting digitally produced video, was so clear and crisp and focused that you could suddenly see every wrinkle on the newscaster's face. It was unnerving. This was partly because lens manufacturers had emphasized improving detail and focus over many years, to overcome some of the inherent flaws of celluloid tape, and the numerous flaws of VHS. Lenses became ever sharper and clearer, as sharp as glass would allow. And then, when digital removed the veil of analog, what was captured looked cold, harsh, sterile, and naked. It took another several years before television stations switched out for softer, more beautiful, hand-ground lenses, and used diffuse lighting and production techniques, and the full potential of digital could start to be realized.

In audio production a similar trend occurred, but it took longer to realize that purity was a flawed point of view. Our bodies respond to audio in a magical way - our ears quickly adjust and become accustomed to the sound. That is why experienced engineers have to take so many breaks, and 'shock' their ears to re-calibrate frequently. Digital seemed to bring in a panacea - computers could measure distortion, frequency response, decay over time, and equipment could be tuned to try to reach some state of perfection the human ear could never achieve. The story of the introduction of digital technology is every human story in a nutshell. An innovative development, immediately misunderstood, over-trusted, and over-estimated. No one could see any downside to switching everything over during the digital fever of the 80s and 90s. We no longer had to rely on, and could be fooled by, our bodies and our ears. We now had science. So, relying on their eyes instead of ears, engineers aimed for purity of waveform and a whole generation of music became sterile, thin, cold, harsh, and unemotional sounding.

Why? Well obviously low distortion was not a good substitute for good audio. What we are beginning to understand is that 'distortion' is a term that covers a gigantic category of audio colors. Each recorded sound has texture, weight, heft, smoothness, and shape. Silky, creamy, hefty, thumpy, hairy, weighty, dark, thick, syrupy, etc. All of these characteristics fall under what audio engineers until quite recently called 'distortion'. There are many audio characteristics that don't even have names yet.

During the early years of the Renaissance, in Italy, paint colors were made from pigment ground by hand. Some colors, like the beautiful lazurite, were imported from far away - lazurite came from Afghanistan, from mined lapis lazuli that was like a deep ocean blue. That color was so rare and special the Catholic church had placed a ban on using it for anything other than religious art (it was used for Mary's veil). All pigment-based paint was rare and expensive, so only the elite could paint, commissioned by the wealthy. But then into the 1700s synthetic colors began to make their way into the markets, especially Prussian blue, derived from iron cyanide. Prussian blue was discovered by accident, but it opened up a whole avenue of discovery. Synthetic colors began to become cheaper and more accessible, and this free availability of colors laid the groundwork for the explosion of the expressionists, impressionists, and finally abstract artists of the early 1900s. These artists were not wealthy or elites, but rather common people who stumbled onto a love of color, which had become freely available to everyone in European society. By the time of Rothko, who painted only in blocks of dissolving color, cost and availability was of no hindrance, and almost infinite colors were available to painters, thus infinite emotion.

In the same way, digital recording technology is just now becoming freely available to everyone. Recording technology used to be the domain of big budgets, big names, overblown songs and lots of drugs. Now, audio technology has become more and more available to anyone who wants to use it, and is even starting to become affordable. As it does we are seeing small companies popping up to provide the iconic sounds of the big studios of yesterday - for example I have clones in my budget studio of the hand-wired 1176 FET compressor and the 70s pop rock Trident equalizer. What made both of these pieces of equipment special was not their original purpose, which was squashing audio and moving frequencies around. What made them special was the coloration you could get out of these devices. You could push them and drive them, and within a certain range you could get a wide variety of tones and textures of sound. The 1176 compressor makes things thick and thumpy and metallic, like a hard-hitting 70s drum set, or a chunky Stephen Stills acoustic guitar. It came in many variations and they all sound different. The Trident 80b equalizer thickens up the midrange with a crunchy texture and makes the upper-mids sparkle, like a Rod Stewart acoustic guitar, or every single instrument in a Cake song (think of 'Never There'). These are two extremely different types of 'distortion', and the distortion was really a side-effect of attempting a completely different mechanical process, namely compression and EQ. What if we actually focused all our effort on understanding what this universe of distortion is and how we could control it?

'Upper mids sparkle' - these kinds of descriptors are terms audio engineers use, as we often break up the audio spectrum into lows, highs, and mids, and smaller segments in between. The human ear can hear approximately 20 hz, which is the lowest rumble, to 20 khz, the highest whistle. For comparison, dogs can hear to 40 khz. Our upper range of 20 khz is quite high, but our range of greatest sensitivity is the range of 2 khz to 4 khz, the upper mid, where much of the intelligibility of the human voice and tonal emotion lies. Then we hear the rest of the midrange, from 150 hz to 2 khz, as different kinds of warmth and color.

Our brains zoom in on these ranges and magnify it. This full range of 150hz to 4khz is basically the range of what you hear through a laptop speaker, or through an iPhone, or any single-speaker per channel device like the car, headphones, and most portable devices. The interesting thing is that engineers used to mix focused primarily on this range ("mix for the midrange") in the 60s and 70s, but then as home speakers (and cars with subs) became more full range there was a trend to mix to the highs and lows. Music began to sound bigger and brighter, but sometimes big and emotionally lacking, because the midrange didn't speak out with clarity. The midrange carries the emotion. Emotion is art. Clarity of emotion is the highest of art.

But now, as the phone revolution has taken off our brains have zoomed back in on this range because we listen to everything again on very small speakers. These speakers need an emotional midrange to grab onto. Color has suddenly become much more important. It's the music with highs and lows rolled off. It's the live or die by your emotion range. And many of the most classic pieces of gear treat this range of frequencies with special color. Even beyond qualities like texture and density there is an unknown frontier of movement, as certain beloved pieces of gear create special movement within recorded audio, like the Helios F760 compressor which helped create the sucking and exploding signature Led Zeppelin staircase drum sound.

I do believe digital has the potential to open up a new age of audio engineering excellence, it may be just beginning now. And we have much to learn. The one thing we have begun to learn in audio, just as in video production with searching out the most beautiful lens glass, is that digital recording gives us the capability of capturing beauty in exquisite detail. Potentially infinite detail. Which means there is a potential for infinite complexity. Which means there is potential for infinite beauty. Which evidence shows lies in the midrange of music.

Beauty of texture, shape, density, weight, heft, punch - beauty of emotion. We are just beginning to understand how different audio colors can shade the emotion of an album. The sound of Nick Drake, that woody intimate thumpy sound, is the sound of the Sound Techniques recording console in Chelsea, England. The console was handmade by Geoff Frost and his partner John Wood, because they had a dream of making a recording studio in Chelsea but had very little money to buy one. Richard Thompson and Jethro Tull albums from that era have a similar woodiness of sound, because they recorded and mixed albums through the same console. This woodiness is a color, an emotion, a sense of intimacy, it brings a feeling of trustworthiness, a sturdy, solid, deep feeling. It actually flows out of the handmade product of Frost and Wood, it's their audio soul in a way, and now its captured. That's one audio-color, what should we call it? How about sturdiness? I imagine a time in the future where an audio engineer will think, "These drums need to sound more sturdy," and reach for that color.

We have no idea how many categories of audio color even exist. A recorded sound is a three-dimensional form. It's height and depth are formed by the frequencies, high and low. It can sit from front to back, in front of the speakers or behind. It can have a rounded shape, a boxy room shape, or a modern open diffused shape. The texture of the sound is a world unto itself, and it can vary by frequency. The API sound that personifies the 70s is pleasantly boxy, with a thick cardboard thump in the low-mids and a papery texture to the high-mids, gently saturating and rolling off the highest frequencies. It has a thick, gooey, textured feeling, compared with more neutral-sounding gear. API gear takes the midrange of a sound, the most human part of the sound, and expands it in our ears moving all of the details forward in a rounded presentation. Can that whole description fit under 'distortion'? No, and so it becomes apparent a new language is needed.

The special power of digital technology is its brilliant transparency. Digital recording allows you to add layer upon layer transparently. So audio could be crushed, twisted, turned, and layered upon itself a thousand times over without much negative side effect. A song could be played into a room and recorded through a microphone, into a thousand rooms and a million microphones, and layered over itself again and again. The combined capabilities of audio color and transparency of digital recording technology are beyond imagination. A new renaissance of music could begin. Music in a fourth dimension could be created, the way we reacted with shock when the first paintings with depth and realism were created, layering audio onto itself in many iterations of emotional complexity. The combined emotion is deeper than could even be imagined because of the densely layered beauty.

We could imagine the invention of glazing, it would have brought a revolution to a world of only clay ceramic pots, sometime around 8000 - 9000 BC. A pot for thousands of years was the color of the clay, always. Now suddenly it could become blue, or blue shading into brilliant red. And then, over time the quality and variety of glazes increased, first alkaline and then tin styles of glazing were developed. They soon began to experiment with layers of varying kinds of glaze, to achieve greater depth and dimension. The same process will begin to unfold in digital audio engineering, with digital capabilities finally providing a tremendously transparent modern glaze of unending audio texture. What we could accomplish with this new technology has not even been thought of yet.

All of that feels complex, but it's just the icing on the cake of a good song. Excellent engineering can make a good song sound incredible, but first you need a good song. In a good room, played by highly sensitive fingers, with a good ear. Another way to put it is this: a $100 special horsehair paintbrush is not going to make a difference to an amateur, but in the hands of Van Gogh it will make all the difference in the world. And so it is with any piece of music gear. But still we will chase the gear, because of its affiliation with magic, and we love talismans. It's rare to find a producer who can understand the technical concepts, and also has a free enough mind to create originally. That's rarely found in the same person. Tom Dowd, Tchad Blake, Rick Rubin, Nigel Godrich, and George Martin are examples of technical competence with creative brilliance.

The best audio engineers, all the ones I listed above, are highly creative people who simply had fun with the gear. They played, all the time, whenever possible. And that is really the secret to becoming a master at anything with music - find something that resonates with you, where time passes quickly and you become lost in the moment, and then play with it all the time and have fun. Until you eventually master it.

Some of the most fun I've had with audio engineering has been playing around with delays and reverb, especially the mechanical ones that use real tape or real springs. Artificial reverb came about because if sound engineers wanted a vocal to sound like it was in a room after it was recorded, they actually had to play it back in a room and re-record it, which became a common practice. They began to build echo chambers for that purpose. In the late 50s an innovative German audio company (EMT) came up with the first big development in reverb - basically a 4 by 8-foot giant metal plate that you could play sound through and record the resonance. Plates could be tuned so that the reverb could sound very large and wet, or short and dense, and engineers had many tricks to get plates to sing out in particular ways. None of them sounded the same. The washy metallic resonance you hear bathing the vocals on songs of the 60s and 70s is mostly plate reverb.

Similar to plates, but taking up way less room, were the lowly spring reverbs, often included with electric guitar amplifiers from Fender. This was simply a long metal spring in a metal tube, the sound was played through the spring and the reverberations were captured by a little microphone. My first spring reverb was amazing because it was a real physical object. You could bang on the side, and it would sound like a tree falling in a canyon and echoing forever. I like spring reverbs on vocals because they have a little metallic grit, a dirtiness, to their sound which makes it grab on and help the vocal sit in the mix with all the other instruments.

Music is really all about listening. To those who are willing to listen well, much will be unfolded. Mastering guitar comes out of playing guitar often, listening very carefully to each note, and being present in the moment. Lately I've been playing by turning my head to the side, close to the wood of the guitar, and from there I can tune my fingers to get a beautiful balance of attack, sustain, and release.

Before recording get a perfect balance by ear in the room. Then, start with the diaphragm of the microphone where the ear was, record, and see how that sounds. Play with a matrix of many different microphone placements and emotional styles, and then listen back and think about which style and technique meshes together and best represents the emotion of the song. The key here is volume. Try a bunch of stuff, take a break, listen back, and try more stuff. When tracking, it's useful to have a small speaker on hand, one that cuts out the top and bottom. The little Auratone speaker is famous for pushing out the midrange, and that's the kind of speaker you should be listening to when playing around with microphone placement.

The microphone is simply a diaphragm that is picking up reflected sound in the room, so try to make every surface sound beautiful. Natural materials, and no hard-right angles. Think about how our ears would hear reflected sound in a wood house, or a hut, or a cave, or the woods - complex overlapping surfaces of natural materials. It's the sound of shelter, protection, human habitation, family, meaning, and community. The other surface that sounds beautiful is the human body. Just putting another body near the microphone, or stretching out your own body in a different way, will make the reflected sound more warm and intimate. We feel and absorb the warmth of sound reflected off of the human body. The next level above that could be movement. A warm body rocking you might be a transcendent sound. Either way the principal applies - humans respond emotionally to the sounds of our primal adaptations, of nature. Would an acoustic guitar, played gently rocking, in front of a fire, be the most beautiful sound? Once you start thinking along this thread it leads to many creative experiments.

My advice for any young audio engineer: learn to connect your ears to your emotions, and then trust your instinct from there.

ADVICE ON CREATING

To begin to create you must begin with truth about yourself, your behavior, your desires, your place in the world, and your story. You cannot obscure this, you must descend into it and understand it. If you always live your life on the stage, you cannot understand what play you are in and you cannot audition for a different play. In this way we need to confront what path we have been on. Examine it with clarity and objectivity, even if it hurts. Sometimes our family or culture set us on a destructive path we know we can no longer walk. These paths are in the past. We turn to see our own path, and then turning back we can see other pathways begin to open in the forest.

Looking requires courage. You will feel rising resistance. Your shadow side will likely try to hide aspects of your own path from view. Primal parts of our unconscious want to keep us trapped in the moment, never looking back or pushing forward. The eternal child, never really comprehending the impact of our actions; the dragon. But the path of the artist is truth, all truth that can be seen must be seen and understood. To see a path is to see a story unfolded, a small mythology, and the path we can see most clearly is our own. We see the human condition in our condition, so we must look and understand. Although each path is different they are all fundamentally human, and so we learn the ways of paths by studying our own.

Look also at your deepest desires. What sets your heart on fire, what gets you daydreaming, what sensations do you love, what are your furthest dreams, what dreams have you put away? Look deep into your shadow, your dark side. What terrible things have you done this year, things you don't like to think about or look at? Who have you wounded? What terrible things did you say or do to someone long ago? Moments of the shadow, moments of shame. Look at them and understand them, why you did what you did, letting them integrate into you, dissipating the barriers in your unconscious. Dissolve into your emotions, so you begin to feel whole again, all feeling coming back in a rippling wave. Note that this process takes a lifetime.

Sometimes to look like this requires we paint, or sculpt, or write our pain and darkness, dreams and fears. That way we can abstract our expression and get around our resistance. In *The Artist's Way* one of the fundamental concepts is writing the 'morning pages' - just filling three pages with writing every single morning. No matter what there is to say, just write, no choice. It will mostly be terrible, narcissistic stuff, and that's fine, it's for no one else but you. Write every single day. Eventually the haze surrounding the question 'who am I' will begin to lift. Within the writing you can see yourself emerge and become more and more clear over time. Emotional clarity, which can equal power, confidence, assuredness, and rightness.

Out of the unconscious comes many ideas, all different kinds. It is primal. Don't let it surprise or shock you. Dragons are below. But this is not the 'real you' any more than the other layers are the real you. Ideas arise out of the unconscious, as if bubbling up from the depths. Over that layer is the censor, which we usually have engaged at all times to ensure we are acting in a correct way. And then on top of that is our conscious observation of what we are creating and feeling. For the purposes of creating music we want to learn to relax the censor temporarily and let ideas flow, keeping a pulse on our emotional response while keeping our fingers musically connected to our emotions.

Distracted focus is what some researchers have called this state. It's basically the classic idea that arises in the shower. I have found that I get the most ideas when my body is doing something physically rote. My body goes into automatic mode, like when taking a shower, driving to work, eating breakfast, or working in the garden. Working in the garden or doing something with my hands creates a positive feedback loop. I capture little ideas while I work to accomplish something I can actually stand up and look at and feel good about. "There, I have three new ideas and all the weeds are out."

Moving the idea into a different 'domain' can help focus on it with a different lens. For example, a rhythmic idea might feel originally expressive, but the melody is repetitive and derivative. So I will sometimes take the rhythmic idea and turn it into syllables, or nonsense words. Then play with tones around the syllables, experimenting. Try it on piano, then on guitar, try voice together with bass; just play. Make up hooks, then string the hooks together, then reverse them. Play until the melody is highly original and evokes emotion as deeply as the rhythm. Then put the words back in and put it all together. In this way you can separate each scale of view, each lens can be changed out according to your purpose as the master artist.

Your unconscious is very influenced by your emotions and your environment. So as an artist you are responsible to create a world conducive to a relaxed state of mind, which gives the creative brain room to roam. Silence works for some. The modern world is so full of noise, silence alone can be jarring to the left brain causing it to surrender to the right. For others it may be drone, jazz, folk, or ambient music. I recommend just a loop of Indian tanpura drone. Our body resonates and our tempo decreases with the music, the mind relaxes and the unconscious comes to the forefront. The primal tempo is slower than our modern tempo. Inhabit your body and be present in your senses. Feel and listen.

This slowing of the tempo to be fully present is a practice that can distinguish a good from great artist. A master artist inhabits movement that is slow but exponentially expressive. Emotion connected to craft. For nine seasons PBS's *Art 21* has filmed artists simply doing their work, and one unifying factor that stands out to me is the slow intentionality with which they create. There is a joy in the action of the moment, creating, in which they can be fully present. This concept goes across many cultures, from meditation to mindfulness. Different expressions of a similar mode of being. But with the artist the presence is purposeful: to inhabit with life each moment of creation.

Having descended into the psyche, pick up your craft and play with it for a little while. Inhabit the moment and tease out a new expression, a new way of making something. The creative brain loves finding play, like a child, so this is often the most painless way to get in the flow. Play with your craft until you are finding a groove in both mood and skill. Then, from that place, connect the fingers to the unconscious and begin to create slowly. Try to stay in flow, maintaining direct connection to the emotion.

For myself, I've found it takes at least an hour to fully descend and slow my tempo to where I can finally listen. Until then I'll be playing with my guitar, warming up my voice and generally playing with different emotional tones. Once in that state, I can finally start playing in a useful way with the end intention of creating something new. Once I finally reach that state I can be extremely productive. I've found that if I get distracted and shift my focus onto something else, if I lose the emotional train of thought, then when I come back I sometimes have to start back at the beginning. But if I can stay in that mode then I can begin to follow a winding path through the woods, the trees arching overhead. If in the woods I stumble on an idea I immediately record it with my handheld recorder or phone. The emotion is what I need to capture, and sometimes the ephemeral emotion can change or be lost if I wait even a few minutes. "I'll always remember that in the morning" - that philosophy became the bane of my existence until I stopped staying it. But if I capture the emotion then I can easily recreate it and remember exactly what was special about it. Further down the path, I take that emotion and slowly play with it. Making it more complex, more syncopated, slowing it way down, trying different seated positions. Looking for moments that resonate my soul deeply, I slowly turn it over and over. Always going back to the original recording to make sure I haven't lost emotion.

A music idea will often start with some nonsense words, or half-formed lyrics, that seem to fit the phrasing and the emotion. Then, I will come back later when I'm in a more critical state, and critique my lyrics separately. Do they speak succinctly, with power, as if they were their own condensed little poem? By separating the lyrics from the musical emotion, I can polish them with greater focus and with a poet's critical lens, and then re-combine them with the music and see the emotional synergy surge. This process - separating one aspect of the craft and focusing on it until it is beautiful - can be very useful.

The clarity with which craft can convey emotion will depend on the skill of the artist in connecting the two, but also will depend on the ability of the artist to feel the emotion clearly. Bravely the artist descends to wrestle with the unconscious. The flow is like lava, unfiltered, and the power depends on clarity of the felt emotions and the ability of the artist's craft to express them. Disconnection from the body, disconnection from emotion, these are things that block the artist.

I played piano for ten years before picking up guitar in college. On piano I could noodle, I could arrange, I could even go easily into moments of arpeggiated transcendence. But I could not write with originality, for some reason everything came out sounding like something else. It was not until I took up guitar in college that I could write with direct connection to emotion. Piano theory had formed itself into grids in my mind, forever stuck in the left brain, grids always preventing my fingers from connecting fully to my unconscious. I knew no guitar theory, which turned out to be highly beneficial for creativity, so I maintained that ignorance. Guitar for me is always an exploration into the dark, no grids to catch my fall.

When I first began to write original music it felt like trying to row blindfolded across an unpredictable ocean. I was full of insecurity and constantly blindsided by waves of emotion. I would become immersed in a new song idea for hours or days, elated, caught up in the inebriation of my new creation, convinced it was the deepest song ever written – it would change the world. But then later, in the cold light of day, I would hate what I had made, tearing up the pages I had written and feeling ashamed of all my delusions of grandeur.

The first time I played an original song for someone else I was at a park, with a young lady. We were on a blanket in the grass. It was a beautiful warm day, I was strumming my guitar, and I figured it was now or never. She fell asleep halfway through the song. I was inwardly crushed, ashamed, and I chastened myself for being so vulnerable. The first few years of writing songs followed this pattern. I would pursue a song idea for days or weeks, only to despise and discard it later. I couldn't trust myself. My first few albums were wrapped up in this complex web of insecurities. Then slowly, over time, I began to connect more directly to my whole unconscious and could begin to feel the 'rightness' or 'wrongness' of an idea. I began to learn how to catch myself early, before heading too far down a wrong path. And I began to learn how to release my creation without judgement or shame – it was simply my soul at that moment in time.

It's a careful balancing act, the art of critiquing yourself without crippling yourself. I believe every artist who tries to create with originality will go through some version of this process. The only way to reach the other side is to walk through the valley, wrestle with yourself, reach a point where you can release your art, and then move on. Over time the blindfold dissipates and you will feel and see more clearly what is a true expression of your soul in realtime as you create.

The simplest pathway to making transcendent art once you have perfected your craft is to create at a high volume and then be very selective. Stanley Kubrick would shoot prodigious takes of the same scene, and later review them in the comfort of his home studio. Out of those many takes, one might have a special magic. Do that for every single take in the movie, and you have a magical piece of cinema. Sounds simple, but it is quite difficult. First you have to be endlessly creative - he would try anything and everything during those takes, pushing the actors beyond their limits. Then you have to develop your eye, or ear, or potentially all senses and whole body, in some way to allow you to understand what is moving art. You have to have clarity of emotion, intuition in service to craft. However, this process, once perfected, can be quite joyful - you are just in the moment for all of these creative impulses, and then you slowly review and refine them later, listening to the body and the soul for impact.

Over time, once you have perfected this technique, the beauty of it is how secure you feel. A lot of fear of creating is an aversion to being judged too soon, when it's not ready yet. But in seclusion, working on ideas, there is no one to judge. The sheer volume permits a level of certainty. I know that within all of those takes one of them was truly transcendent. And if each take is transcendent, then all of those takes put together will create transcendent art. Transcendent art is created when every component is transcendent.

This principle of volume has applied directly for me in arranging and mixing my own music. When recording new music I expect to try many many things, many of which will not work. And I am present in the process of trying, experimenting, searching - it's all expected and good. I might try a harmonica, mute it and try an organ, mute it and layer some vocals. I'm staying in a creative flow while trying many things, keeping connected to my body and emotions for what moves me. Then I might unmute the organ and vocals together and try to get a blend through volume automation. Then I take a break and come back and see if I still agree.

Volume requires motivation, and that can be a struggle. You will certainly not feel inspired all the time. However, the artist side of you, the playful creative side, is not very sophisticated. It's more like a little child. So you can kind of trick it, or hack it. That side of you is very affected by your story, so literally just tell yourself a story of your life. End it with where you want to be. Visualize yourself having achieved that goal, but do not let the height of the goal overwhelm you. Rather, think of it instead as a path, and so you must walk today's part of the path. If you do that every day you will go to great heights. Just start on the path and walk it again tomorrow. Tell yourself, "just for six months"...knowing once you get in the habit you're golden. You gotta be tricky.

That is much easier said than done. Your inner child can be stubborn and lazy. I found that I was wasting a tremendous amount of energy by procrastinating, feeling guilty, and eventually feeling anxious and panicked enough that I made myself create. That is a cycle of defeat - procrastination>guilt/shame>avoidance>anxiety/panic>do-something-poorly> beat-yourself-up-for-it>more procrastination. But you can break the cycle by getting ahead of it. Don't procrastinate. Figure out what time of day you are most productive and block out that time. Then when the time comes just start, don't hesitate, think of how good it will feel to get something great done. Focus on that feeling and then go into the zone. Set the ambiance and tone and make your own little world. Using this method you can become highly productive. I recommend you consider whether your digital devices are helping or hurting your art.[1]

Remember to be in the moment and enjoy the moment. To be able to create any kind of art we want is truly a blessing of our modern life. We need to be thankful for that and enjoy the process.

NOTES

1. Channel 4 News. Jun 15, 2018. *Jaron Lanier interview on how social media ruins your life.* https://www.youtube.com/watch?v=kc_Jq42Og7Q

2. Traver, Teresa Huffman. *Flannery O'Connor: Spiritual Writings.* Orbis Books, 2004.

3. Campbell, Joseph. *A Joseph Campbell companion: Reflections on the art of living.* Joseph Campbell Foundation, 2011.

4. Rothman, David J. "'Divinely Superfluous Beauty': Robinson Jeffer's Versecraft of the Sublime." *Robinson Jeffers: Dimensions of a Poet.* Fordham University Press, 1995.

5. Nietzsche, Friedrich. *The Twilight of the Idols.* Jovian Press, 2018. (Orig. 1889)

6. Rothko, Mark. *Statement on the Artist's Attitude in Painting,* 1949. https://www.rothkocenter.com/en/about-rothko/statement-about-art

7. L'Engle, Madeleine. *Walking on Water: Reflections on Faith and Art.* Convergent Books, 2016.

8. Rank, Otto, and Charles Francis Atkinson. *Art and Artist: Creative Urge and Personality Development.* AA Knopf, 1932.

9. Withy, K. "Situation and Limitation: Making Sense of Heidegger on Thrownness." *European Journal of Philosophy.* 2014.

10. Hackforth, Reginald, ed. *Plato: Phaedrus.* No. 119. Cambridge University Press, 1972.

11 Tarnas, Richard. *The passion of the Western mind: Understanding the ideas that have shaped our world view.* Random House, 2010.

12 Durant, Will, and Monica Ariel Mihell. *The Story of Civilization Volume 1.* Simon & Schuster, 1935.

13 Durant, Will. *The Gentle Philosopher.* http://will-durant.com/

14 Priestland, David. *Merchant, Soldier, Sage: A New History of Power.* Penguin, 2013.

15 Frankl, Viktor E. *Man's Search for Meaning.* Simon and Schuster, 1985. (Orig. 1946)

16 Gordon, David J. *Iris Murdoch's Fables of Unselfing.* University of Missouri Press, 1995.

17 Mill, John Stuart. *Autobiography of John Stuart Mill.* Columbia University Press, 1960. (Orig. 1873)

18 Maslow, Abraham H. *The Farther Reaches of Human Nature.* Arkana, 1971.

19 Murdoch, Iris. *The Sovereignty of Good.* Routledge, 2013. (Orig. 1970)

20 Rumi, Jalal al-Din. *The soul of Rumi: A New Collection of Ecstatic Poems.* Harper One, 2002. (Coleman Barks, Trans.)

21 Muir, John. *The Yosemite.* Modern Library, 2010. (Orig. 1912)

22 Piff, Paul K., et al. "Awe, the Small Self, and Prosocial Behavior." *Journal of Personality and Social Psychology.* 2015.

23 Emerson, Ralph Waldo. *Nature (1836).* Ed. Kenneth Walter Cameron. Scholars' facsimiles & reprints, 1940.

24 Campbell, Joseph. *Pathways to bliss: Mythology and personal transformation.* New World Library, 2004.

25 Durant, Will. *Story of Philosophy.* Simon and Schuster, 1961. (Orig. 1926)

26 Nietzsche, Friedrich. "Schopenhauer as Educator." *Untimely Meditations.* 1874. (D. Pellerin, Trans.)

27 Dobrowolski, Irek (Director). 2018. *Struggle: The Life and Lost Art of Szukalski*

28 Cummings, Edward Estlin. "A Poet's Advice to Students". *A Miscellany (Revised).* Liveright Publishing, 2018. (Orig. 1955)

29 Holsten, Glen (Director). 2018. *Wyeth.*

30 Underhill, Evelyn. *Mysticism.* London: Methuen, 1911.

31 Cameron, Julia. *The Artist's Way.* Penguin, 2016. (Orig. 1992)

32 Maslow, Abraham Harold. "A Theory of Human Motivation." *Psychological Review.* 1943

33 Lewis, Clive Staples. *Surprised by Joy: The Shape of My Early Life.* Houghton Mifflin Harcourt, 1995. (Orig. 1955)

34 L'Engle, Madeleine. *The Rock That is Higher: Story as Truth.* Convergent Books, 2018. (Orig. 1993)

35 Starbuck, Edwin Diller. *The Psychology of Religion: An Empirical Study of the Growth of Religious Consciousness.* Walter Scott, 1899.

36 John. *The Collected Works of Saint John of the Cross.* ICS Publications, 1991. (Orig. 1584)

37 Csíkszentmihályi, Mihaly. *Flow and the Psychology of Discovery and Invention.* Harper Perennial, 1997.

38 Katahira, Kenji, et al. "EEG correlates of the flow state: A combination of increased frontal theta and moderate frontocentral alpha rhythm in the mental arithmetic task." *Frontiers in Psychology.* 2018.

39 Lehrer, Jonah. *Imagine: How Creativity Works.* Houghton Mifflin Harcourt, 2012.

40 Nietzsche, Friedrich. *The Twilight of the Idols.* Jovian Press, 2018. (Orig. 1889)

41 Broughton, Simon (Director), Dalrymple, William (Writer). 2005. *Sufi Soul: The Mystic Music of Islam*.

42 Asimov, Isaac. "Isaac Asimov Asks,"How Do People Get New Ideas?"." *MIT Technology Review*. Massachusetts Institute of Technology. 2014.

43 Badman, Keith. *The Beatles: Off the Record*. Omnibus Press, 2009.

44 Dowlding, William J. *Beatlesongs*. Simon and Schuster, 2009.

45 Jones, David. *The Aha! Moment: A Scientist's Take on Creativity*. JHU Press, 2012.

46 Tolstoy, Leo. *What is Art?*. Penguin UK, 1995. (Orig. 1897)

47 Greene, Robert. *Mastery*. Penguin, 2012.

48 Campbell, Joseph. *The Hero with a Thousand Faces*. New World Library, 2008. (Orig. 1949) *Image from Wikimedia Commons. 'Sourced from Reddit and redrawn by User:Slashme'*

49 Gruen, John. *The Artist Observed: 28 Interviews with Contemporary Artists*. A Cappella Books (IL), 1991. (Francis Bacon, Orig. 1972)

50 Ellsberg, Robert, ed. *Flannery O'Connor: Spiritual Writings*. Orbis Books, 2003.

51 Prideaux, Sue. *Edvard Munch: Behind the Scream*. Yale University Press, 2007.

52 Taylor, Christa L. "Creativity and mood disorder: A systematic review and meta-analysis." *Perspectives on Psychological Science*. 2017.

53 Holm-Hadulla, Rainer M., Martin Roussel, and Frank-Hagen Hofmann. "Depression and creativity—The case of the German poet, scientist and statesman JW v. Goethe." *Journal of Affective Disorders*. 2010.

54 Johnston, Daniel. *Hi How Are You*. 1983.

55 Flaherty, Alice Weaver. *The Midnight Disease: The drive to write, writer's block, and the creative brain*. Houghton Mifflin Harcourt, 2015.

56 Perogamvros, Lampros, et al. "Friedrich Nietzsche and his Illness: a neurophilosophical approach to introspection." *Journal of the History of the Neurosciences*. 2013.

57 Didion, Joan. "In Bed". *The White Album*. Macmillan, 1990.

58 Blom, Jan Dirk. "Alice in Wonderland syndrome: a systematic review." *Neurology: Clinical Practice*. 2016.

59 Saner, Emine. 'I tried to drill a hole in my head': how Lydia Ruffles recovered from unbearable migraines. *The Guardian*. Mon 13 Aug 2018.

60 Seaburg, Maureen. The Red of His E String. *Psychology Today*. Feb 21, 2012.

61 Nietzsche, Friedrich Wilhelm. *Beyond Good and Evil*. Boni & Liveright, Inc. 2018. (Orig. 1886)

62 Camus, Albert. "The minotaur, or the stop in Oran."; "The myth of Sisyphus". *The myth of Sisyphus and other essays*. Knopf. 1955.

63 Bergman, Ingmar, and Marianne Ruth. *Images: My life in film*. Arcade Pub., 1994.

64 Huxley, Aldous. *Proper Studies*. Chatto & Windus, 1933.

65 Egan, Keith J., ed. *Carmelite Prayer: A Tradition for the 21st Century*. Paulist Press, 2003.

66 Jung, Carl Gustav. *Psychology and Religion*. Yale University Press, 1960.

67 Dutton, Denis. *The Art Instinct: Beauty, Pleasure, & Human Evolution*. Oxford University Press. 2009.

68 Yaden, David Bryce, et al. "The Varieties of Self-Transcendent Experience." *Review of General Psychology*. 2017.

69 James, William. *The Varieties of Religious Experience*. Longmans, Green and Co. 1902

70 Rodman, Selden. *Conversations with Artists*. Devin-Adair Co., 1957.

71 Zuckerman, Gabrielle. *An Interview with La Monte Young and Marian Zazeela.* American Public Media. http://musicmavericks.publicradio.org/features/interview_young.html
The Tortoise, His Dream and Journeys: https://www.youtube.com/watch?v=bapAGrWpaLw

72 Ghosh, Dipak, et al. "Tanpura Drone and Brain Response." *Musicality of Human Brain through Fractal Analytics.* 2018.

73 Lustenberger, Caroline, et al. "Functional role of frontal alpha oscillations in creativity." *Cortex 67.* 2015.

74 Budzynski, Thomas. "Tuning In On The Twilight Zone". *Psychology Today.* August, 1977.
https://www.futurehealth.org/articles/Tuning-In-On-The-Twilight-by-Tom-Budzynski-100129-958.html

75 Curcumia, Rusudan, and Joseph Jordania. *Echoes from Georgia: Seventeen Arguments on Georgian Polyphony.* Nova Science Publishers, 2010.
http://www.josephjordania.com/files/55-USA-comparative.pdf

Selected videos:
Svaneti: https://www.youtube.com/watch?v=xAKz_5iiCT4
           https://www.youtube.com/watch?v=z_JfFIUGEOA
           https://www.youtube.com/watch?v=7bB_GDDAy7s
Kakheti: https://www.youtube.com/watch?v=ifOY55ncqIE
           https://www.youtube.com/watch?v=0rgnII-FdD8
           https://www.youtube.com/watch?v=e6TEyvLxT0Y
Kutaisi: https://www.youtube.com/watch?v=lgZvbAcFhcQ
           https://www.youtube.com/watch?v=R5uYO_XLpKA
           https://www.youtube.com/watch?v=26ScAbGPqac

76 Lanois, Daniel. *Soul Mining: A Musical Life.* Farrar, Straus and Giroux. 2010.

www.ingramcontent.com/pod-product-compliance
Lightning Source LLC
Chambersburg PA
CBHW030655220526
45463CB00005B/1779